# Earth Science

### Discovering the secrets of the earth

# LANDFORMS

*Atlantic Europe Publishing*

# ◈ *Atlantic Europe Publishing*

First published in 2000 by
Atlantic Europe Publishing Company Ltd
Copyright © 2000
Atlantic Europe Publishing Company Ltd

**Author**
Brian Knapp, BSc, PhD

**Art Director**
Duncan McCrae, BSc

**Editors**
Mary Sanders, BSc and Gillian Gatehouse

**Illustrations**
David Woodroffe, Simon Tegg and Julian Baker

**Designed and produced by**
EARTHSCAPE EDITIONS

**Reproduced in Malaysia by**
Global Colour

**Printed in Hong Kong by**
Wing King Tong Company Ltd

**Suggested cataloguing location**
Knapp, Brian
Earth Sciences set of 8 volumes
Volume 6: Landforms
1. Geology – Juvenile Literature
2. Geography – Juvenile Literature
550
ISBN 1 862140 58 8

**Picture credits**
All photographs are from the Earthscape Editions
photolibrary except the following:
(c=centre t=top b=bottom l=left r=right)
Prof Denys Brunsden 13tr; NASA 11, 12t, 13bl, 15b,
51t; USGS 7 (Austin Post), 51t.

This product is manufactured from sustainable managed
forests. For every tree cut down, at least one more is
planted.

# Contents

*Chapter 1:* Landforms and the rock cycle     4
   How the landscape changes     6
   Land building     7
   Erosion     13
   Deposition     15

*Chapter 2:* Jointing and weathering     18
   Sheeting and jointing     18
   Weathering     22

*Chapter 3:* The importance of rock structure    26
   Cap rocks     26
   Natural staircases     28
   Waterfalls     30
   Dipping beds     32
   Landscapes of folded rocks     37
   Domes and basins     40

*Chapter 4:* Rocks at the coast     41
   Caves, arches and stacks     41
   Discordant and concordant coasts     44

*Chapter 5:* Landforms from faulting     47
   Fault scarps     47
   Rift valleys and horsts     48
   Transcurrent faulting     50

*Chapter 6:* Landforms of igneous rocks     52
   Volcanic landforms     53
   Dykes     58
   Sills     59
   Batholiths     59

Glossary     60

Set Index     66

# *Chapter 1:* Landforms and the rock cycle

LANDSCAPE – the shape of the earth's surface – is all around us. We see it in terms of mountains and hills, plateaux and plains. But, as varied as the landscape appears to be, there are, in fact, patterns in the way in which the land has been shaped. These patterns appear on all scales. For example, valleys sculpted by glaciers, such as Yosemite Valley shown in the picture on the right, often have the same characteristic 'U' shape.

But, there are also grander patterns to the way in which the land is shaped, patterns that we cannot readily see from the ground. If you look at the earth from space, for example, you will find that each continent is made up mainly of wide plains and narrow belts of mountains and hills. So, the landforms of the Yosemite landscape are part of a grander landscape of mountain belts, which run along the entire length of western North America.

These grander features are not randomly placed over the earth's surface but are the result of the way in which the earth works. Mountains are produced – by a process called MOUNTAIN BUILDING – when TECTONIC PLATES collide. They always form elongated mountain belts at the edges of the existing continents. Thus each new mountain range adds a strip of land to the core of the continent against which it forms. Plains usually occupy the centres of continents; they are rarely disturbed and have taken a long time to become worn down. They are mostly very old. (You can find out more about the subject of plate tectonics in the book *Plate tectonics* in the *Earth Science* set.)

In this first chapter, therefore, we will set out the grand design for the world's landscapes, explaining how mountains and plains are formed, how the earth's rocks are added to, and how they recycle constantly. In later chapters we will look more closely at the

(Below) This picture shows the mountain landscape of the Yosemite Valley, California, USA. It contains a number of types of scenery – valley and mountain. Each type of scenery is made up of a number of distinctive landforms. In the distance there is the peak of Half Dome, a landform created by a region of rock more resistant than its surroundings. All of the rocks here were formed deep within an ancient mountain belt and have only been exposed by a long period of erosion. The shape of the valley is, in part, the result of erosion by rivers and, more recently, by glaciers. The floor is flat because it is the sediment of an ancient lake bed. But, the shape of the cliffs is controlled by the fault lines which cross the rocks, presenting some directions that are easier to erode than others.

landscape to see how patterns or textures of rock help influence the patterns of landforms on a more local scale.

# How the landscape changes

Each time new mountains are built, they are gradually worn down – ERODED – to plains. Erosion strips away rocks that are softer much faster than those that are harder. In this way the landscape becomes more varied. Thus, as mountains are worn down, the patterns of rocks they contain become exposed and contribute to the wide range of scenery.

Geologists can recognise many distinctive features in any landscape. Each feature, for example, a cliff or a gorge, is called a LANDFORM. Patterns of the landforms made up the scenery.

As some landforms are eroded, the eroded material, called SEDIMENT, is carried by water, ice, and wind and perhaps deposited elsewhere, making new landforms such as deltas and coastal beaches or river floodplains and desert sand dunes.

Most of the sediment laid down on land or in the sea will be covered by more sediment in turn. The weight of this new material will compact the sediment

*(Below)* This diagram shows the main features of the land surface. Mountain ranges form on the edges of continents, where intensive folding and faulting occur, but the folding occurs on a lesser scale beyond the mountains to create ranges of hills. The interiors of the continents are not affected by folding and consist of level sheets of sedimentary rocks covering ancient crystalline rock.

Rivers and ice sheets erode the land, and transport sediment to the nearby plains and to the sea. This material builds up and eventually consolidates as new rock. Much will later be crushed into new mountain belts.

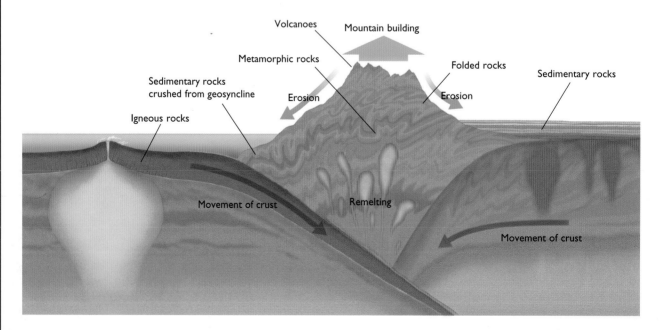

below it, while minerals dissolved in the water squeezed out of the sediment will be deposited as cements between the grains. In this way, material eroded from the land will very slowly be changed into new rock.

Eventually, much of this new rock will be uplifted to form new mountains, and these new mountains will then be eroded once more. This cycle of erosion, sedimentation, rock formation, and renewed uplift is called the ROCK CYCLE.

# Land building

The land is built up in two ways: by the addition of new material from within the earth, as volcanic LAVA and ASH on the surface, or as congealed MAGMA within the earth's crust; and from the reworking of material that has been eroded from an earlier land, deposited as layers on the ocean floor, and lifted up again.

*(Below)* Volcanic eruptions are a sign that new material from below the crust is being added to the earth's surface. The volcano is a landform in its own right, made of layers of ash and lava.

Many kinds of uplift are possible, and most are connected to the collision of tectonic plates.

During a collision, land and ocean floor may be crushed as well as lifted up. This is mountain building. Elsewhere, land may simply be lifted up. This creates plains (close to sea level) and plateaux or tablelands if the uplift is great.

When plates collide, the crust is put under great stress, so that many lines of weakness develop in, and near, the edges of the colliding plates. At the same time, plate collision often results in one plate being forced below another, so that it is pushed down into the MANTLE. This process is called SUBDUCTION. As the subducted plate goes into the mantle, huge amounts of it melt (producing IGNEOUS ROCK). This molten rock rises very slowly as plumes of magma. The process may take millions of years. Magma plumes eventually cool within the crust to form huge bodies of GRANITE called BATHOLITHS.

When the magma is close to the surface, the lines of weakness in the brittle crust allow some of the magma to flow quickly to the surface, where it produces VOLCANOES. (For more information on volcanoes see page 52 and also *Earthquakes and volcanoes* in this set.)

Where volcanoes are common, they, and the plumes or magma chambers that supply them, often add considerably to the bulk of new mountains. Volcanoes can erupt huge amounts of lava and ash which spread out into sheets and layers on the surrounding land, building one on top of another, creating huge plains, plateaux, or tall mountains.

However, volcanic activity is only responsible for chains of islands in the ocean and for isolated volcanic mountains on land. It is never fully responsible for the

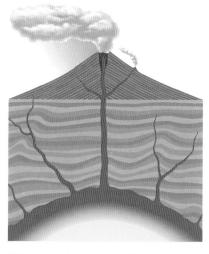

*(Above and below)* Volcanoes that erupt lava send out liquid rock that congeals on the earth's surface in thin sheets. This is new material from the mantle. Floods of lava may fill in old valleys and create new plains, thus creating new landforms.

bulk of large mountain chains. Most of the material in a mountain chain is made from sediment that was once lying on the bottom of the ocean floor, often in a deep offshore trough called a GEOSYNCLINE.

Within this geosyncline, the weight of overlying material turns the sediments into SEDIMENTARY ROCK well before the sediments are crushed up into mountains. As the plates collide, the sedimentary rock is squeezed, some of it downwards into the upper mantle (the ASTHENOSPHERE), and some of it rises as new land.

How the rocks react to immense crushing depends on the intensity of pressure they experience. To understand this, think of a layer of rock as being like a slab of toffee. Rocks that are close to the surface will be cold, hard and brittle and will tend to crack when they are disturbed by any kind of pressure

*(Above)* This cliff section of the flanks of a volcano in Hawaii shows how the volcanic landforms are built up of layer upon layer.

(just as a cold slab of toffee is brittle and cracks easily). These rocks will remain as sedimentary rocks, and usually they will break, resulting in FAULTING.

Rocks that are buried more deeply will be hotter and under more pressure. Just as warmed toffee will start to bend, so, too, hot rocks will tend to bend rather than to break. The result is FOLDING.

In the heart of a new mountain belt enormous forces are brought to bear, and folding may be of extraordinary intensity, with great slabs of folded rocks even being torn from their roots and carried for long distances. The heat and pressure will change the character of the rocks completely, causing sediments to begin to melt and recrystallise, just as the toffee slab will begin to flow when it gets close to its melting point. These are called METAMORPHIC ROCKS, and although they were pliable when they formed, once the mountain building is over and the pressure is reduced, they can become extremely hard.

As mentioned above, the collision of plates causes huge volumes of rock to be crushed. The crust is changed from being flat layers of sediment to being composed of tightly folded belts that are of great thickness. Some of the thickness will be seen in the gradual rising of a mountain belt.

But there is another important reason why mountain belts are high, why they have extraordinarily long lives, and why they take so long to erode to plains. Collisions force as much rock down into the mantle as they force up above ground. However, the mantle is made of much denser rocks than the sediments of the crust. As a result, just as a block of ice floats on water unless it is held down, so the mountain belts will tend to float on the mantle below. Thus, at the end of the collision, mountains continue to rise despite their immense weight. And, just as an iceberg keeps the same proportion of its height above the surface of the water as it melts, so a mountain belt keeps the same proportion of its bulk above the mantle as it is worn away. Thus, as

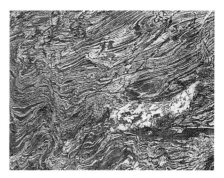

*(Above)* Under the intense pressure and heat of mountain building, rocks bend and fold easily, as shown in this example. The picture shows a piece of rock about two metres across.

*(Right)* This space shuttle picture shows a part of the Nepalese Himalayas drained by the Arun River, a tributary of the Ganges.

The river cuts many deep gorges through the high mountains of the Himalayas (top of picture), then it flows in a wide, braided floodplain across the Ganges Plain (bottom of picture). Here, it deposits huge amounts of gravel, sand, silt, and clay to build up the level of the Ganges Plain.

Despite this loss of material, enough sediment continues to be carried by rivers to form the giant Ganges-Brahmaputra Delta in the Bay of Bengal, and even more sediment is carried beyond the delta to be laid down on the ocean bed.

In this way, erosion in one place is linked to sedimentation in many other places. The landforms that are created in the process are the result of the action of the weather, rivers, and ice on rocks. Both erosion and sedimentation are part of the rock cycle.

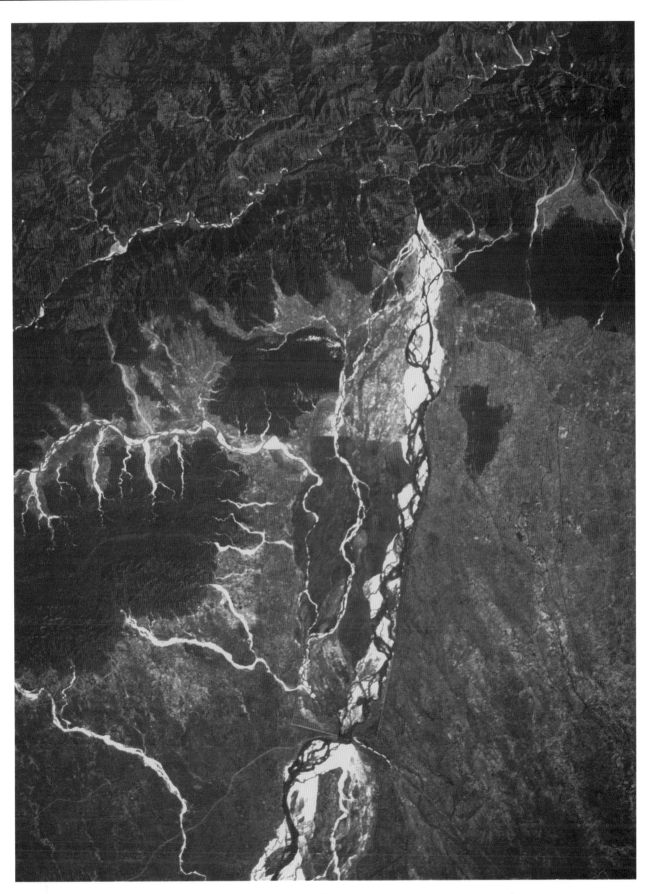

mountains are eroded, they weigh less heavily on the mantle and rise.

The rising never quite balances out the loss in height due to erosion, but it explains why mountains have such long lives. To erode a mountain belt requires the removal of the mountains you can see and the mountain 'roots' you cannot.

The effects of a tectonic collision can occur many thousands of kilometres from the zone of impact. Thus, a large part of a continent may rise a little. This may produce a land of broad swells called domes separated by basins, or it may result in regular ripples of the crust. Rocks that are arched upwards make ANTICLINES, and those that are arched downwards make SYNCLINES.

*(Above)* The Zagros Mountains, Iran, showing ridges and valleys that exactly follow the pattern of folding of the rocks. The long, winding anticlines make the mountain ridges, while the synclines form the valleys.

In the process of folding, the crests of the folds are weakened. This makes them more vulnerable to erosion. In this desert environment, erosion has had only a limited effect, but elsewhere the ridges can be stripped off completely, as shown in the Appalachian Mountains on pages 37 to 40.

# Erosion

No part of the rock cycle ends before another part begins. Thus, throughout the time new mountains are being formed, agents of the weather are at work removing them. This is called EROSION.

Rivers, glaciers, and waves soon cut into the rising mountains and hills, revealing their long-hidden structure. Erosion acts more quickly on the softer rocks, and so they form valleys on land or bays by the sea. The harder rocks remain as mountain ranges or hills and as coastal headlands.

As the uppermost rocks of a new mountain belt are stripped away, the core of the mountain range is exposed. This is when hard, metamorphic rocks are seen at the surface.

(*Above*) In the steep Himalayan valleys, rockfalls are a common means of erosion. Here you can clearly see how material eroded from high on the mountainside can reach the river, where it can be worn down into smaller pieces and then be carried to the sea.

(*Left*) The mighty Himalayas (with Mount Everest in the centre) are a balance between uplift of the land and erosion by agents of the weather. The mountains are rapidly being eroded by glaciers, although the continued rise of the range compensates for this.

After even more erosion, deep-seated igneous rocks (for example, granite, which represents the remains of magma chambers) are exposed and become an important part of the surface geology.

All of these mountain core rocks are very hard, and so erosion is slow, with the hardest rocks, or those with the fewest weaknesses, standing proud as peaks and ridges.

*(Left and below)* These diagrams show how the pattern of rocks in a mountain belt changes as erosion goes on. The landscape changes on different scales. The diagram on the left shows the changes to a mountain belt, while the diagram below shows changes to a single valley in the mountains.

In the early stages the rivers and glaciers cut down into the mountains, creating a complex of peaks and valleys. As erosion continues, the bands of harder rocks are revealed as elongated ridges.

With further erosion, the folded rocks are removed, and the metamorphic rocks begin to dominate the landscape.

As the mountains are eroded down to plains, the granite of the former magma chambers comes to the surface.

In this way the erosion of a mountain belt gives rise to many types of landscape, not just in height, but also in the pattern produced by the rocks.

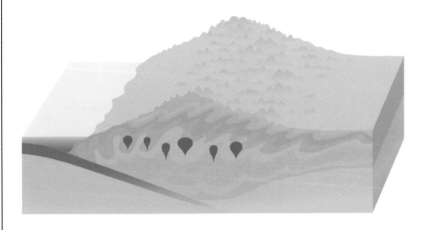

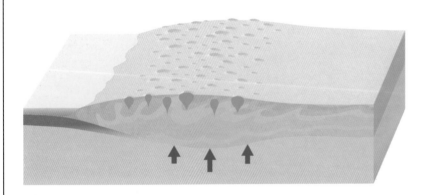

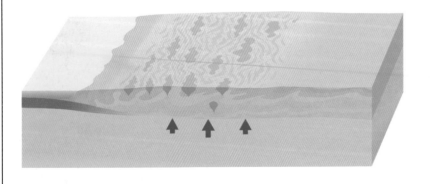

Finally, these rocks, too, are worn down, and a landscape of low relief is formed. Nothing is now left of the mountain ranges except the metamorphic and granite cores. The former mountain range becomes part of the continental heartland, or SHIELD.

# Deposition

Just as erosion takes place throughout the time that mountains are rising, so deposition always accompanies erosion. Thus, the rock worn down from the mountains builds up elsewhere, for example,

*(Below)* This is the delta of the Indus River in Pakistan. Here sediments eroded from the distant Himalayas are being returned to the sea. Some of the sediments make up this vast delta, but the majority are carried out into the Indian Ocean, where they settle out to form sheets of new rock.

as DELTAS where fast flowing rivers enter the great stillness of the sea.

Material carried to the sea by rivers or blown into desert basins by the wind is mainly deposited in layers. Each layer is connected to what is happening on land. If the rivers are rushing down from tall mountains, then the material they carry will be coarse and may settle out to form a CONGLOMERATE. If the rivers are flowing from basins that are mostly dry, but which have periods of torrential rain and floods, then the rivers will be sandy, and the material they bring to the sea will form a SANDSTONE. If rain is common, then soils will form, and the material reaching rivers will be mostly mud. It will be carried to the sea and form SHALES.

The weather changes not just yearly but over decades, centuries, and millennia. And as the weather changes, the material brought by the rivers may also change, so that sandy material may be replaced by muddy material or vice versa. Sometimes there may be no sediment at all, and then the remains of marine animals may be the only material accumulating on the sea bed. When this is the case, LIMESTONES form.

Each layer of sediment becomes buried as more materials accumulate on top of it, compacting it and

*(Below)* This diagram shows the places where sediments build up, both on land and in the coastal zone. At the foot of mountains lie alluvial fans that can eventually be turned into conglomerate rocks. In the floodplains of the rivers are sands and muds that can make layers of sandstone and shale. The desert basins are filled with sands that can make thick sandstone beds; along the coast sandy beaches can form sandstones, while the muds settling in deeper areas of oceans can form shale.

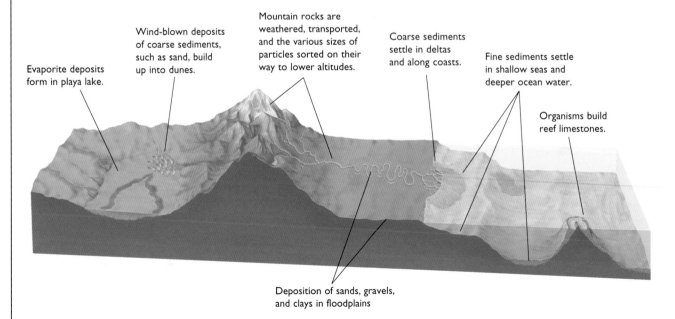

Evaporite deposits form in playa lake.

Wind-blown deposits of coarse sediments, such as sand, build up into dunes.

Mountain rocks are weathered, transported, and the various sizes of particles sorted on their way to lower altitudes.

Coarse sediments settle in deltas and along coasts.

Fine sediments settle in shallow seas and deeper ocean water.

Organisms build reef limestones.

Deposition of sands, gravels, and clays in floodplains

squeezing out the water. If the water is rich in dissolved materials, such as calcium carbonate, iron oxide, or silica, these materials may be left behind to form a cement, which binds the rock particles together. The variety of cements adds yet more variety to the composition of the rocks.

The rock cycle is now complete, for the sediments building up again can now be transformed into new mountains. Everything is in place and simply waits for the next uplift from forces deep within the earth. And, the result of the cycle is that each of these new rocks will have properties that will influence the way in which they are eroded into new, distinctive landforms.

*(Above and below)* Each kind of rock, in combination with the geological history and erosion of the area, produces the landscapes and landforms around us. *(Above)* This mountain of granite is the top of an ancient magma chamber. *(Below)* This is a limestone cliff that follows the line of an ancient fault.

# *Chapter 2:* Jointing and weathering

One of the most important influences that rocks have on the shape of the land is through their natural weaknesses. There are two quite separate effects that together determine how weaknesses in a rock will develop and therefore how it will stand up to erosion. The first is the pattern of cracks that appear in most rocks, and the second is the cements, if any, that hold the grains of a rock together.

## Sheeting and jointing

Most of the rocks we find on the earth's surface were formed deep within the crust. Sedimentary rocks, for example, are formed by being buried under great thicknesses of sediment. They become compacted as water is squeezed out of them, and the grains become cemented together as minerals dissolved in the water are deposited around them.

Metamorphic rocks are formed deep within mountain belts where the heat and pressure are so great that not only are the rocks compacted, but also

*(Above)* As basalt cools, it fractures into hexagonal columns. As the overlying weight is removed by erosion, the joints between the columns become wider.

*(Below)* These granite blocks have been weathered very little. The granite fractured as the overlying beds were eroded away. The blocks make a landscape feature called a tor. Most of the blocks still fit together closely.

new crystals begin to form and interlock.

Some igneous rocks may flow over the surface of the earth, building up layer upon layer into very thick sheets. But huge volumes are squeezed between existing rocks to make SILLS and DYKES, and even larger quantities cool from magma chambers and then cool as giant granite batholiths.

All of these processes produce rocks that are compacted under great pressure. But eventually, once the rocks are lifted up to make mountains, hills, or tablelands, erosion strips layer after layer of rock away.

The effect of removing the weight of overlying rocks is very important. With less weight on them, the rocks are under less pressure, and they begin to expand. But, rock is very brittle, and so it does not expand evenly but rather breaks up into blocks. The gaps between blocks are called FRACTURES.

*(Below)* Sheeting of granodiorite batholiths in Yosemite National Park, California, USA.

If they run parallel to the surface, they may allow the rock to break up into sheets. This shows very dramatically on many granite batholiths, for example. In a sedimentary rock, the sheets are called beds, and the fractures often occur between beds along the surfaces called BEDDING PLANES that separate one bed from another. If fractures cut across the beds of a rock, they are called JOINTS.

Whatever the nature of the fractures, they are lines of weakness that can be exploited by the

(*Left*) This shale breaks naturally into thin sheets along bedding planes, as erosion of the overlying rocks brings it close to the surface. This is not a form of weathering but simply fracturing as the rock expands when the overlying weight is removed.

(*Below*) These fins of sandstone in Arches National Park, Utah, USA, show the influence of fracturing very dramatically. The sandstone bed was formed over a bed of salt. As more beds were deposited on it, the pressure on the salt bed made it bulge upwards, arching the rocks above it as well. However, the overlying rocks were brittle, and so they fractured right across. Now exposed at the surface, the sandstone fractures have been exploited by the agents of the weather. Each fin represents the centre of a block, and each gully is where the rock fractured and has been eroded away.

weather. For this reason, massive rocks with few joints usually resist the weather more effectively than heavily fractured rocks. For example, the rapid breakdown of a shale rock is not because the rock is especially soft; it is simply that shale is criss-crossed with a huge number of fractures. Moreover, because shale breaks up into sheets, the fractured sheets easily slide over one another and so are readily removed.

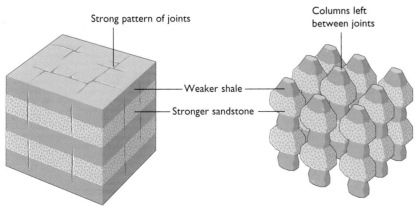

Strong pattern of joints

Columns left between joints

Weaker shale

Stronger sandstone

*(Above and left)* At Bryce Canyon, Utah, USA, soft rocks of different weaknesses lie horizontally on top of one another. The strata are broken up by a system of vertical joints. Weathering has exploited the joints to create columns in the landscape. The irregular shape of each column picks out the difference in resistance of each bed to weathering.

# Weathering

Rocks may appear to be hard, but over time the agents of the weather begin to attack them, finding even the tiniest weakness and exploiting it to the full. Over many years, even the hardest rock begins to show signs of pitting on the surface, and small pieces begin to flake off. The decay of rocks in this way is called WEATHERING. Weathering turns rock into soil and allows it to be carried away by agents of transportation, such as rivers and waves. Two kinds of weathering occur: mechanical and chemical.

## Mechanical weathering

Mechanical weathering happens when a rock breaks up into smaller pieces. The levering action of frost is the most common way in which this happens. It does not change the composition of the rock.

(*Below*) Rainwater can seep into fractures in rock. When the temperature falls below freezing, the water turns to ice. This happens first at the surface, so that the water becomes sealed into the fracture. As it turns to ice, the water expands, levering blocks apart if they are next to a cliff face. This is the most important form of mechanical weathering and is called ICE WEDGING or FROST SHATTERING.

Ice

Loosened block

# Chemical weathering

Chemical weathering is the result of the chemical reaction of water and rock. It creates new chemical substances, some of which are soluble and are carried away by the water, while some are insoluble and remain behind as fine particles, called soil.

Chemical weathering is much more sensitive to rock type than mechanical weathering. Mechanical weathering of a heavily fractured sandstone and limestone, for example, would produce much the same result. But water reacts with limestone to produce only soluble materials. Chemical weathering literally dissolves limestone away. On the other hand, chemical weathering on sandstone simply dissolves the cement that holds the sand grains together. The sand grains are made of quartz, which is stable in the presence of water.

*(Below)* This picture shows the effect of chemical weathering. All that remains is the core of this boulder. The boulder has rotted away as water reacted with the minerals. The rotted material can still be seen surrounding the core as shells. If the shells are touched, they crumble away.

(Right) Pillars of light-coloured volcanic ash are all that remain after a long period of chemical weathering along vertical joints. These are in Chiricahua National Monument, Arizona, USA.

(Below) The exposed upper surface of a bed of limestone. It is called a limestone pavement because it resembles a surface made of paving slabs. The joints in the rock have been etched out by chemical weathering, exposing the shape of the blocks. This is Malham Cove, England.

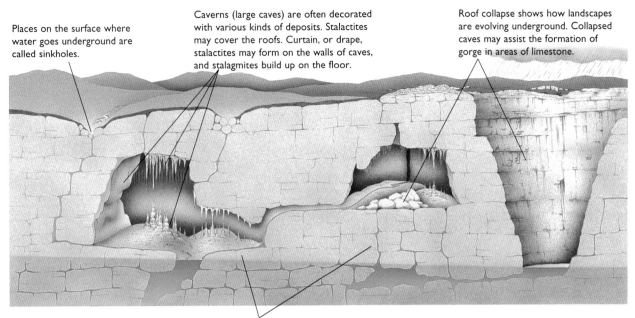

Places on the surface where water goes underground are called sinkholes.

Caverns (large caves) are often decorated with various kinds of deposits. Stalactites may cover the roofs. Curtain, or drape, stalactites may form on the walls of caves, and stalagmites build up on the floor.

Roof collapse shows how landscapes are evolving underground. Collapsed caves may assist the formation of gorge in areas of limestone.

Percolating water exploits the joints in the rock structure, dissolving the limestone and forming a system of tunnels with underground rivers.

*(Above)* Underground and surface landforms of massive limestone.

# Weathering and climate

Chemical weathering is most effective in places that are warm and humid, for chemical reactions need water, and they mostly work fastest at higher temperatures. Chemical weathering works least effectively in dry climates.

Mechanical weathering works best with climates where the temperature hovers around freezing, for the most important agent of mechanical weathering is ice. To force blocks of rock clear from cliffs, the fractures between blocks have to be filled with water, and then the temperature has to fall and allow ice to form. Thus the most effective climate for mechanical weathering is one where rain is common, which experiences frost every night, but which warms up again during the day.

Neither mechanical nor chemical weathering is very effective in places where it is permanently hot and dry, or where it is permanently below freezing.

*(Above)* Carlsbad cavern system, New Mexico, USA, is one of the world's largest. The stalactites hanging from the ceiling of the cave show clearly in the foreground, while stalagmites rising from the floor can be seen lit up in the background.

# *Chapter 3:* The importance of rock structure

Depending on the history of a landscape, rocks may have beds that are horizontal, that slope at an angle, or that arch over in a fold. In all cases the nature of the beds – the structure of the beds – can play an important role in affecting the shape of the landscape.

## Cap rocks

Horizontally bedded rocks have an important influence on the landscape when one rock layer is very much more resistant than those above and below it. The rocks above become weathered and eroded away, leaving the resistant rock as a topping on the landscape. Cap rocks are commonly made of limestone, sandstone, and sheets of lava.

Landscapes with cap rocks are most dramatic in desert areas. Here, the cap rock is slowly eroded away to leave a wide range of features.

Typically, in an arid landscape, rivers first cut canyons through the cap rock, which are then widened. As widening occurs, some of the plateaux between canyons can become isolated. This produces a MESA. Mesas are reduced in size more quickly because erosion now occurs on all sides. Mesas are then eroded to smaller features called BUTTES, which are reduced, in time, to needle rocks, pillars, and pinnacles before finally being eroded away. However, during all this time the cap rock remains, so that, although the features get smaller, they always keep the same height. The Colorado Plateau in the southeastern United States provides one of the world's best cap rock landscapes. This plateau includes the famous area known as Monument Valley.

*(Below)* This massive band of basalt caps the cliff and provides the sheer drop in the upper section of the cliff. It is the Isle of Skye in Scotland.

*(Below)* A cap rock provides particularly striking landscapes in areas of desert. Occasional flash floods cut gorges into the land surface, and horizontally bedded rocks are dissected into tablelands and isolated features called mesas and buttes.

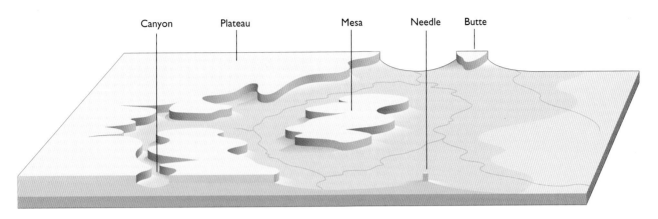

Canyon · Plateau · Mesa · Needle · Butte

*(Below)* An aerial view of the Monument Valley area showing a mesa in the middle of the picture and buttes in the foreground.

*(Below)* A bed of massive sandstone caps this plateau landscape in Monument Valley on the Arizona/Utah border. On the left is a mesa. The relatively small isolated feature to the right of the picture is a butte. In the distance is a needle rock.

Mesa · Needle rock · Butte

# Natural staircases

When beds lie horizontally in the landscape, erosion invariably produces a natural staircase, with the most resistant rocks forming cliffs (the rises of the staircase) and the less resistant rocks forming the treads. This is most pronounced in places with little vegetation cover, such as in deserts and at the coast.

Where beds of massive hard rocks occur, the cliffs are usually vertical. Here, the rock can stand up like a wall. On the other hand, cliffs in weak materials are prone to slumping and gullying. The result is a 'badlands' type of landscape, with the weak rocks heavily gullied or a jumble of slumped material.

In landscapes that have a humid climate, with frequent rain, nearly all rocks weather into soils. This has a dramatic effect on the landscape. Whereas in deserts, and at coasts, loose blocks are weathered

*(Below)* How differences in rock resistance lead to natural staircases.

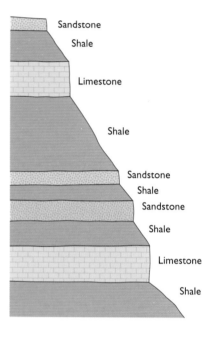

Sandstone
Shale
Limestone
Shale
Sandstone
Shale
Sandstone
Shale
Limestone
Shale

*(Left)* A natural staircase.

and then fall away and so keep profiles sharp. When rock weathers to soil, it forms a blanket of material that masks most of the changes in rock hardness. Horizontally bedded rocks rarely produce dramatic scenery in such climates.

*(Below)* A cliff staircase in the side of a river gorge, Goosenecks, Utah, USA.

# Waterfalls

Some of the world's most spectacular waterfalls are the result of differential erosion in level bands of rock.

As rivers cut through each layer of rock, a tough rock band may prevent the river from cutting down. The river may flow for long distances with very little gradient as a result of being held up on a cap rock.

Below the cap rock are much weaker rocks that are easily eroded once the cap rock has been broken through. Where the river manages to erode through the cap rock, the water falls down to a new level. The lower level of the waterfall is the level of the next hard rock band.

The greatest erosive power is where the water falls. Although the falling water has little direct effect on the hard cap rock, where it falls, it can erode the softer rock below and in this way undermine the cap rock, causing it to collapse periodically. In this way, the waterfall retreats. By contrast, because it is not undermined in this way, the cap rock to either side of the waterfall erodes only slowly. Thus, the cap rock

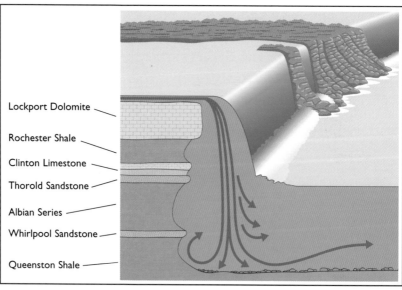

Lockport Dolomite

Rochester Shale

Clinton Limestone

Thorold Sandstone

Albian Series

Whirlpool Sandstone

Queenston Shale

*(Above)* The diagram above shows the various rocks that make up the face of Niagara Falls. The cap rock in this case is a hard carbonate rock called a dolomite (the Lockport Dolomite). Below it lie soft Rochester Shales. Another ledge in the face of the waterfall is provided by the Clinton Limestone, and a further soft rock, the Albian Series, lies below. The river has scoured out a deep plungepool in soft Queenston Shale at the Horseshoe Falls, but it lies under water and cannot be seen.

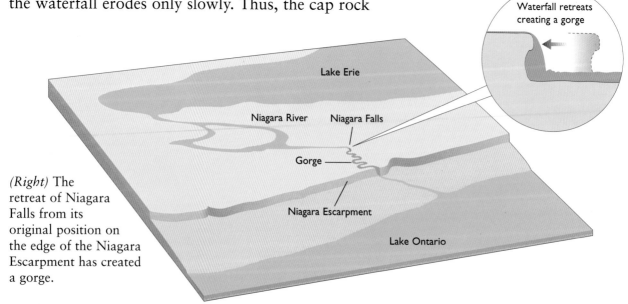

Waterfall retreats creating a gorge

Lake Erie

Niagara River    Niagara Falls

Gorge

Niagara Escarpment

Lake Ontario

*(Right)* The retreat of Niagara Falls from its original position on the edge of the Niagara Escarpment has created a gorge.

*(Above)* The Horseshoe Falls from the Canadian side of Niagara Falls.

erodes back much faster along the course of the river, creating a gorge that marks the position of its retreat.

Cap rock waterfalls make up some of the world's most dramatic waterfalls. Niagara Falls, on the New York-Ontario border, is perhaps the most spectacular example. Here, the horizontally bedded cap rock is made of Silurian limestone.

A wide variety of other materials creates the cap rocks for waterfalls. Bands of igneous rocks, usually as sills or dykes, are common causes of waterfalls.

# Dipping beds

When beds of rock slope markedly, they are said to DIP. The angle of dip is measured down the steepest part of the slope. The direction across the bed, at right angles to the dip, is called the STRIKE.

Dipping rocks create a dramatically different kind of landscape from level rocks. No longer do hard bands of rock make tablelands, mesa, and buttes in the landscape. No longer do waterfalls form. Instead, dipping rocks produce a more varied landscape because the different hard and soft rocks OUTCROP at the surface in quick succession.

Thus, for example, rivers flowing across bands of rock that are dipping form rapids, the water spilling from one hard ledge to a trough made by the succeeding softer one.

*(Above)* High Force Waterfall in northern England has a sill of hard dolerite as its cap rock.

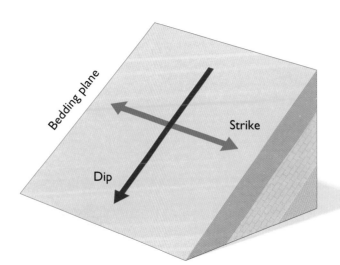

*(Left)* The definitions of dip and strike.

*(Right and below)* As rivers flow over dipping beds, they tend to form a series of rapids rather than waterfalls.

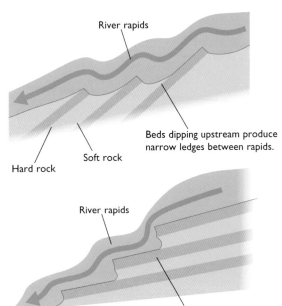

River rapids

Beds dipping upstream produce narrow ledges between rapids.

Hard rock

Soft rock

River rapids

Beds dipping downstream produce wide ledges between each rapid.

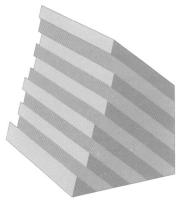

*(Left and below)* Cliffs made in dipping rocks are steep when the beds dip back into the cliff, but more gentle when the beds dip out of the cliff.

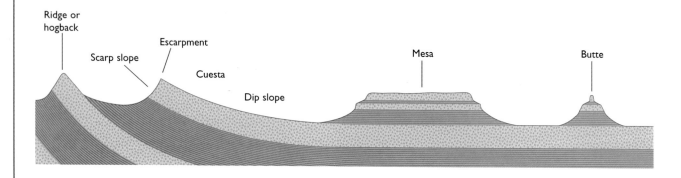

Labels on diagram: Ridge or hogback, Scarp slope, Escarpment, Cuesta, Dip slope, Mesa, Butte

## Cuestas

The succession of hard and soft rocks makes ridges known as CUESTAS and lowlands known as vales or basins. The top of a cuesta is called the ESCARPMENT; the steeper face is called the SCARP SLOPE, and the more gentle slope is called the DIP SLOPE (because it slopes at the same angle of dip as the rocks). Sometimes, rocks will be tilted very steeply, so that the scarp and dip slopes are more or less at the same angle. The ridge that marks the highest part of the rock is often called a HOGBACK.

Cuestas are long ridges across the landscape paralleled by valleys. In general, rivers follow the valleys. But there are important exceptions to this. In many cases, the rivers suddenly turn and cut right through the cuestas, producing a WATER GAP or a WIND GAP if it now has no river flowing through it.

Water gaps suggest that the development of a cuesta landscape is more complicated than might, at first, be supposed.

The diagrams at the top of page 36 show how geology can influence river courses. In the top diagram, rivers develop on a uniform cover rock. It is then eroded away, exposing bands of hard and soft rock below.

*(Above)* This diagram shows how the landscape related to dipping rocks is very different from that of horizontal rocks. Horizontal rocks tend to produce dissected tablelands, while dipping rocks produce cuestas and lowlands.

*(Below)* The landscape of southern England shows a sequence of cuestas. In this case, nearly all of the cuestas are limestone, with the lowland between formed in shales.

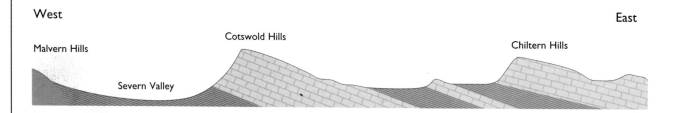

West — Malvern Hills, Severn Valley, Cotswold Hills, Chiltern Hills — East

*(Below)* The pattern of ridges and valleys that is commonly found in a landscape of dipping rocks. The escarpment top and steep scarp slopes are usually forested, while the dip slopes and valleys are often farmed.

Dip slope

Escarpment

Scarp slope

Vale

The dip slope, escarpment and scarp slope all make up a cuesta.

*(Below)* A hogback formed in pink-coloured sandstone.

Escarpment

Dip slope

Scarp slope

The tributaries begin to erode the softer rocks quickly, while the main rivers have difficulty cutting through the hard rock bands. Thus, in time it is the tributaries that flow in wide valleys, while the main rivers often flow through gorges or water gaps.

As the landscape develops further, some of the tributaries may cut back into the valleys of their neighbours, capturing the water from the upper part of the neighbouring basin. This may deprive the captured river of enough water to flow, and so the gap that it had cut through the hard rock dries up and in time is seen only as a notch in the cuesta – a wind gap.

As time goes by, these changes mean that the original vein-like pattern of rivers is replaced by one in which rivers mainly run parallel to the cuestas. This pattern, with many right-angle bends in the river course, is often called a trellis drainage pattern.

*(Below)* These diagrams show how geology can influence river courses.

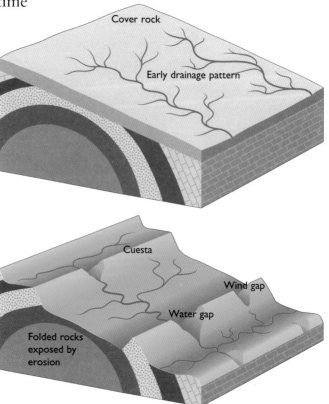

*(Below)* The Susquehanna River, Pennsylvania, cuts through a fold in the Appalachian Mountains, creating a water gap.

# Landscapes of folded rocks

When rocks bend into a pattern of simple folds, the upwards-arching part of the fold is called an anticline, and the downwards part is called a syncline.

Simple folds occur in many places, often being broad swells with only a gradual change in height. This is called loose folding. Tight folds, where the vertical extent is quite large, are less common. Two of the best displayed patterns of such folds occur in the Jura Mountains on the border of Switzerland and France and in the Appalachian Mountains in eastern North America.

*(Below)* The cuestas and water gaps of the Juniata River in the Pennsylvanian Appalachians. Compare the perspective, in contour map and in geological cross-section.

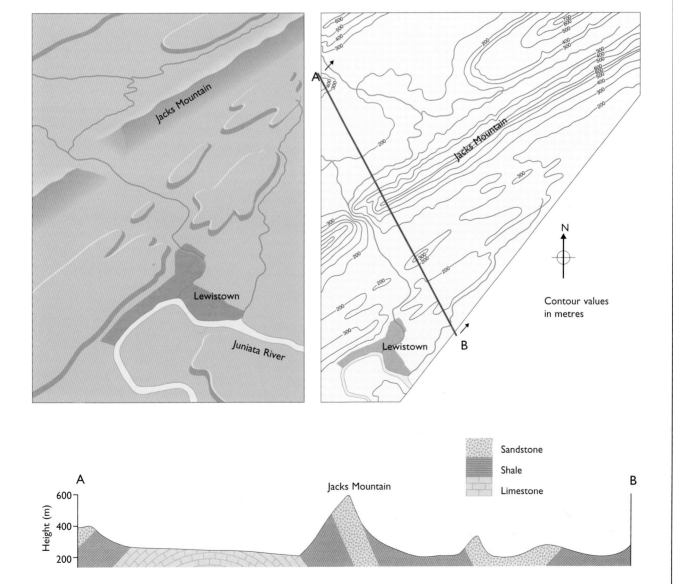

In the Jura Mountains, the anticlines actually correspond to the ridges and the synclines still form the valleys between them.

When rocks are buckled into folds, the folded tops of the anticlines and the bottoms of the synclines are bent more severely than the flanks. The more the

(Below) Pitching folds just south of Harrisburg, Pennsylvania, in the Appalachians show up particularly well in this aerial view. The Susquehanna River cuts through two cuestas in the middle of the picture, thereby making a remarkable U-turn.

(Left) This diagram shows how the erosion of the arched parts of the folds produces a pattern of ridges and valleys.

bending, the greater the pattern of fractures that develops in the rocks.

Many of the crests of tightly folded rocks are therefore less resistant than the flanks of the folds. As a result, tributaries to the main rivers quickly erode the crests of the anticlines and produce narrow valleys. In this way, the crests of the anticlines are opened. Anticlines with the centre of their arch eroded away produce pairs of inwards-facing cuestas.

The line along the top of an anticline or the bottom of a syncline is called the FOLD AXIS. Sometimes the axis is level, but quite commonly the axis dips down into the ground. This produces a PLUNGING FOLD.

Plunging folds are eroded in the same way as level folds, but in this case the inwards facing cuestas begin to converge, so that in plan they appear V-shaped.

The tight folds of the central and northern Appalachian Mountains show this pattern especially well.

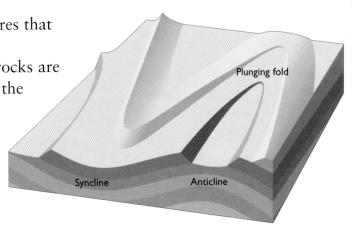

(*Above*) In parts of the Appalachians, the folds slope down, or plunge, into the ground. The ridges then appear to have a V-shaped plan.

(*Below*) As erosion goes on, synclines can sometimes become the highest points of a landscape, as the photograph below shows.

# Domes and basins

When rocks have been folded from two directions, the rocks form into BASINS and DOMES. These are three-dimensional folds. Erosion of a basin will often create outwards-facing cuestas in the form of rings, whereas domes will have rings of inwards-facing cuestas.

The drainage that develops from domes is often circular, with the tributaries forming curving paths as they erode the bands of softer rocks around the rim of the dome.

*(Below)* This Space Shuttle view of the Appalachians, shows an elongated basin (left of centre) among a pattern of parallel folds.

# *Chapter 4:* Rocks at the coast

Waves are the most sensitive of all the processes of erosion. Changes in rock hardness that would not be detected by eye will often be rapidly exploited by the coast.

The main processes at work on a coast are HYDRAULIC ACTION and ABRASION. Hydraulic action is the pressure that waves exert on the rocks when they break directly against them. It is most important when there is deep water against a headland, for example. If the rock is fractured, breaking waves will force both air and water into the cracks. The amount of pressure that builds up is considerable and comes with every breaking wave. The pattern of building and then relaxing pressure occurs relentlessly and eventually causes rock fatigue. In this way, blocks of fractured rock can be pulled from cliffs. In general, the more fractured a rock, or the more frequent its joints and bedding planes, the more it is liable to be attacked. Shattered rocks along fault lines are, for example, particularly susceptible and are often eroded into long, narrow caves.

The other main erosion process of waves involves sand and pebbles carried by the waves. During storms, waves carry a large amount of material and hurl it at the coast. In time this abrades the coastal rocks, wearing them away whether or not they are fractured. Coasts where this process is important often have a rounded, wave-cut notch at their base. This kind of erosion works most effectively when the foreshore is shallow and contains a beach.

## Caves, arches and stacks

As cliffs are worn back, waves scoop out softer or more fractured rocks to make caves and leave harder, less fractured rocks as headlands, arches and pillars – called sea stacks and stumps – standing out at sea.

Sea caves are deep, natural hollows in a cliff.

(Page 42 and below) Coasts often have a variety of caves, arches and stacks in them. These can be used to help identify the rock structure. For example, in the picture to the left, the jutting out rib of rock in the foreground is paralleled by two coves, one on each side. Thus the rocks along this coast must be aligned parallel to this rib. Now look at the isolated stack in the background and see how the shape can, in part, be explained by the way in which the rocks are aligned. However, the caves give another clue. They occur at right angles to the alignment of the rocks, suggesting that there are also lines of weakness present in this direction. Lines of weakness that do not correspond with the alignment of the beds are most likely to be connected with faults.

(Below) Small offshore stumps represent the former position of the headlands.

(Below) In the picture below, which shows heavily fractured rocks which are also made up of thin bands of hard and soft rocks, there is a varied pattern of caves. Where the rocks are more uniform in texture, the caves are rounded. But, where alternating bands of hard and soft rocks dip steeply down to the right, the caves generally extend up and to the left as they parallel the dip. In the larger cave, the line of weakness can clearly be seen extending up to the left from the cave roof.

Many sea caves are tall and narrow. This shows that the waves are eroding a weak band of rock between two bands of tougher rock. Sea caves can form in any rock that is strong enough to support a cave roof without it collapsing.

Natural stone arches form when two caves grow across a headland. When the caves meet, an arch is formed. A sea stack (called a needle if it is very thin and a stump if it is mostly worn down) is formed when the roof of an arch collapses.

## Discordant and concordant coasts

The shape of a coast often tells you a lot about the rocks that the waves are attacking. Coasts with headlands and bays show that the cliffs contain both hard and soft rocks, and that these rocks are steeply dipping, thus allowing many different bands of rocks to be attacked by the waves over a short length of

(Below) This diagram shows how many features of a coastline can be related to the geology. Notice that rocks can be easier to erode either because they are soft (for example, shales and clays) or because otherwise tough materials have been made weak, for example, by shattering along a fault.

Whether a concordant or discordant coast results depends on the relationship between the strike of the rocks and the coast.

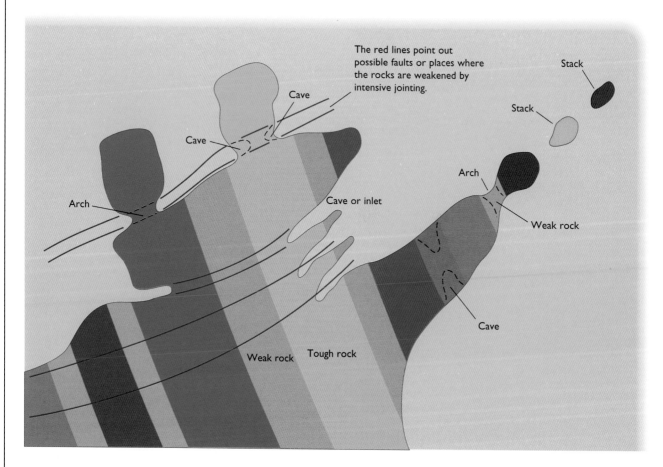

The red lines point out possible faults or places where the rocks are weakened by intensive jointing.

Cave

Cave

Stack

Stack

Arch

Arch

Cave or inlet

Weak rock

Cave

Weak rock    Tough rock

coast. Long, uniform coasts suggest that the rock on the coast is very uniform in character or is made of horizontally bedded rocks.

A headland is always made of rock that is harder than the rocks on either side of it. It has been able to stand up to the battering of the waves more successfully than the rocks nearby.

*(Left and below)* Patterns of fractures in the chalk rock on this discordant coast are picked out by the waves, producing a headland with many erosional features.

Where fractures on the sides of the headland are exploited, caves meet to form arches.

When the roof of the arch collapses, the remaining pillar stands on its own beyond the headland as a sea stack.

The uniform nature of the chalk does not result in any special shape to a cave. Most caves are rounded.

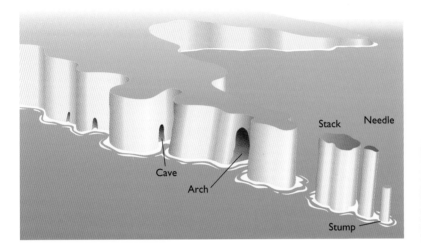

If the bands of rock in the headland run out to sea, the headland rocks stand out to sea as well. Beyond them will be the remains of the headland in the form of arches, stacks, and stumps. It is known as a **DISCORDANT COAST** because the rocks and the coastline are at an angle to one another. It is also the most common kind of coast.

If the coast has few headlands and the bays are rare and clam shaped, it means that the rocks run parallel to the coast. In this case any stacks and arches will not stand out from the coast but will be in the same line as the majority of the coast. It is known as a **CONCORDANT COAST**.

*(Below)* In this example of a concordant coast, the fractures, faults, and lines of shattered rock lie parallel to the coast. As a result, the stacks line up parallel to the shore. Notice that some of the stacks are opposite inlets (places where rocks must be weak), which confirms that the rocks making up the stacks are quite distinct from those on the mainland.

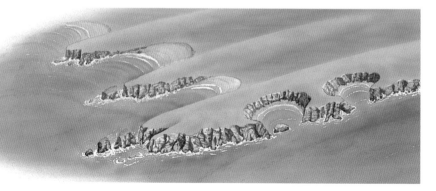

*(Right)* A concordant coast has rocks running parallel to the coast. The coast only displays bays when the tough coastal band of rock is broken through. Once this has happened, any soft rock band lying in-shore will rapidly be excavated back until a new hard rock is encountered. This will often result in clam-shaped bays with almost enclosed entrances.

# *Chapter 5:* Landforms from faulting

The way in which rocks behave under pressure depends on how brittle they are. Deep underground, and confined by a huge weight of rocks above, some rocks change shape easily and tend to bend (fold) under pressure. By contrast, those closer to the surface, which do not have a massive weight of other rocks above them, tend to be more brittle, and therefore snap when under pressure. A major break in the rocks is called a FAULT.

When rocks snap, a large amount of energy is released and is experienced as an earthquake. The amount of movement along the fault is called the DISPLACEMENT. NORMAL FAULTS, where blocks of crust are under tension, most commonly produce landscape features.

Faults may be active for very long periods of time. They are especially active at plate margins. Faults represent deep weaknesses in the earth's crust. They are therefore easy routes for magma to flow to the surface. It is quite common for volcanoes and lava flows to be aligned along faults.

## Fault scarps

A single earthquake may only produce a movement in the crust of between a few centimetres and a few metres. A FAULT SCARP several hundred metres high is therefore produced as a result of repeated faulting. More than this, each time a fault occurs, one part of the landscape is raised up above another, and erosion will therefore be concentrated at this location.

*(Below)* The three main fault types. The red arrows mark the directions of crustal movement, primarily up and down for normal and reversed faults, and side to side for transcurrent faults.

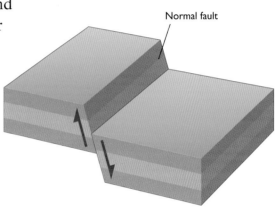

Normal fault

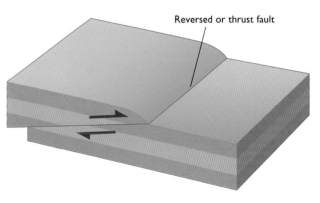

Reversed or thrust fault

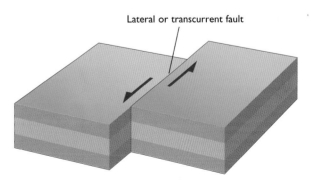

Lateral or transcurrent fault

A fault scarp therefore only becomes visible in the landscape if the rate of faulting is much greater than the rate at which the landscape is eroded. Put another way, the presence of a fault scarp tells of a period of very active faulting and also of rock resistant enough to withstand erosion.

# Rift valleys and horsts

A rift zone is a part of the landscape where the crust has been formed into a broad arch, causing the rocks to be lifted up and at the same time pulled apart. It is also a common setting for fault scarps.

When blocks are faulted upwards, and are bounded on two flanks by fault scarps, they are called HORSTS. When blocks sink, and are overlooked by two fault scarps, they are called RIFT VALLEYS or GRABEN. It is common for both horsts and graben to occur side by side, making a landscape of mountain ranges separated by steep fault scarps from broad lowlands.

*(Below)* Once a fault has been created, the landscape produced depends on the character of the rock. A rock made of weak materials will soon be reduced to a gentle slope, whereas a rock made of hard materials will retain the shape of the fault for much longer.

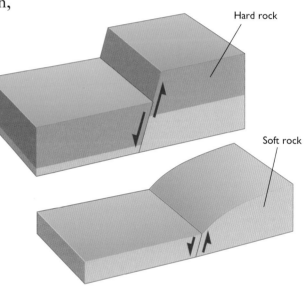

Hard rock

Soft rock

*(Below)* Pressure and tension on rocks can result in both upwards and downwards movement of blocks. The elevated blocks are called horsts; the sunken blocks are called graben.

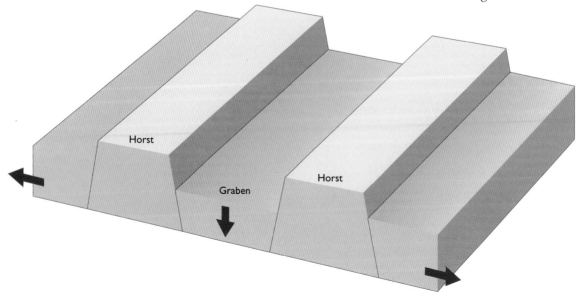

Horst

Graben

Horst

As erosion occurs, the face of the fault scarp is rapidly eroded, so that a sheer rock face is rare. More commonly, rivers cut valleys in the fault scarp, leaving triangular areas between valleys as the last remnants of the faults. These triangular areas are called spurs.

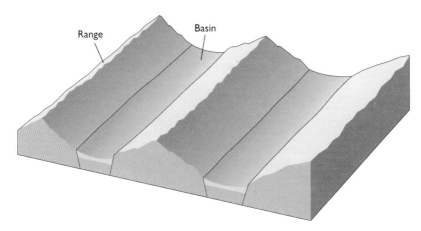

Range    Basin

*(Left)* This diagram shows how uplifted fault blocks, or horsts, and downfaulted rift valleys, or graben, gradually become sculpted by erosion. The features to look for are not the shapes of the mountain peaks – they will often look the same on all kinds of mountain ranges – but the fact that there is a sharp junction between the mountain front and the valley, and that the boundary is straight for the whole length of the mountain range. Notice that the rift valleys fill in with material eroded from the horsts.

*(Below)* One of the world's most extensive areas of horsts and graben occurs in the Basin and Range area of the southwestern United States. About 150 mountain ranges are separated by a similar number of valleys. A famous rift valley in this region is Death Valley in California, where downfaulting has made it the lowest point in the western hemisphere. Compare this picture with the diagram above.

# Transcurrent faulting

Many large and important faults are produced when the earth's plates scrape past one another. Here the movement is sideways, or transcurrent, and there is little change in height. Nevertheless, the effect of the faulting can have major influences on the landscape. This is because the movement shatters a wide belt of rocks on either side of the fault.

Shattered rock is weakened and is therefore more liable to erosion. Transcurrent faults are therefore often picked out in the landscape as long, straight troughs.

One of the most significant ancient transcurrent faults is the Great Glen Fault in Scotland, which is continued as the Cabot Fault in Newfoundland. This fault has a displacement of over 100 kilometres. The shatter belt is matched by a belt of deeply eroded land. It effectively cuts Scotland in two. The shattered rocks were much more easily eroded by glaciers during the last Ice Age, so that a great through-valley (The Great Glen) now crosses the entire country. The Great Glen is partly filled with lochs (lakes), including Loch Ness.

More recently, huge transcurrent faults have formed in California. As with the Great Glen, the

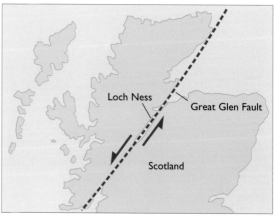

*(Above and below)* The Great Glen Fault can be traced right across Scotland and has played a large role in the shape of the highlands. Loch Ness (seen below) forms part of the Great Glen Fault, its shattered rocks gouged out by glaciers during the last Ice Age.

shattered rocks close to the fault are weaker and so are more easily eroded than the rocks to either side. The weakened rocks of the San Andreas Fault are most easily seen where they reach the coast at Point Reyes, where they have enabled a long trough and inlet to be eroded by the sea.

*(Below)* Point Reyes, California, USA, is an isolated block of rock, separated from the California coast by the San Andreas Fault. The fault line is picked out as the straight line running diagonally across the picture and partly flooded by the sea. It makes the cliffs along a small stretch of coast.

Point Reyes

The picture below was taken from this location with a fault line running straight across the foreground.

# *Chapter 6:* Landforms of igneous rocks

Igneous rocks – those produced from liquid magma upwelling from deep within the crust – can produce a wide range of landforms on an equally wide range of scales.

Some magma cuts through older rocks to produce volcanoes. Volcanic rocks are called EXTRUSIVE. They include the lavas and ashes that make the cones of volcanoes and the great floods of basalt that spread across the landscape from fissures.

However, spectacular though volcanoes are, much of the material that rises up into the earth's crust from the mantle never reaches the surface but cools while still deeply buried in the crustal rocks. Such materials are called INTRUSIVE ROCKS.

*(Below)* The main types of igneous landforms.

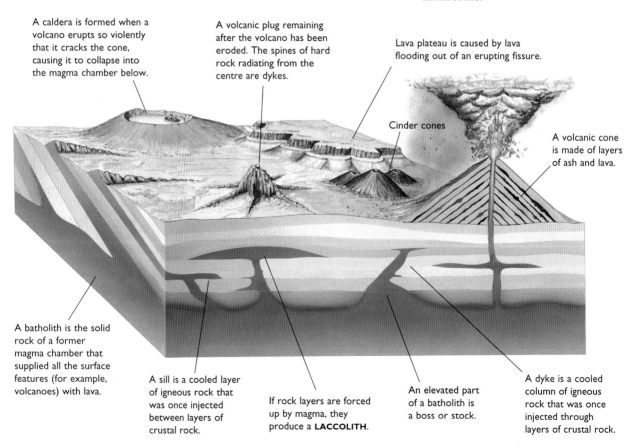

A caldera is formed when a volcano erupts so violently that it cracks the cone, causing it to collapse into the magma chamber below.

A volcanic plug remaining after the volcano has been eroded. The spines of hard rock radiating from the centre are dykes.

Lava plateau is caused by lava flooding out of an erupting fissure.

Cinder cones

A volcanic cone is made of layers of ash and lava.

A batholith is the solid rock of a former magma chamber that supplied all the surface features (for example, volcanoes) with lava.

A sill is a cooled layer of igneous rock that was once injected between layers of crustal rock.

If rock layers are forced up by magma, they produce a **LACCOLITH**.

An elevated part of a batholith is a boss or stock.

A dyke is a cooled column of igneous rock that was once injected through layers of crustal rock.

The largest body of this material is the magma chamber that once fed the volcanoes. It cools slowly to granite. The great mass of the cooled magma chamber is called a batholith. Many batholiths have an irregular upper surface where some magma has risen higher than the main mass. It produces features called BOSSES and STOCKS.

The pressure is very high inside a magma chamber, and liquid magma can force its way across and between the rocks that enclose the chamber. Magma that cuts across rocks and then cools as a wall of igneous rock is called a DYKE. Magma that levers beds of rock apart and then solidifies into a sheet of igneous rocks is called a SILL. Magma can also make rocks arch up, and fill the space to produce an inverted bowl of igneous rock called a LACCOLITH.

Each of these igneous forms has its distinctive impact on the landscape.

## Volcanic landforms

Volcanoes have a variety of shapes depending on the nature of the magma that supplies them. When the crust splits apart and allows lava to flow out along a fissure, no volcanic cone may be produced at all. Instead, a sheet of lava will flow over the landscape. The lava that comes from fissures is normally basaltic, and it is very runny. It moves across the landscape like water, flowing down slopes and filling in depressions and valleys in the landscape. Lava of this kind makes a sheet of rock that may, when exposed in a cliff, for example, look just like any other rocks, except for the fact that it has an igneous, not a sedimentary, origin and can be distinguished by the columns that often form in it.

Basalt is generally harder than sedimentary rocks and often makes a cap rock in the landscape (see page 26).

Not all basalts make lava sheets, and many build up huge, low-angled domes instead. They are called shield volcanoes. The islands in the Pacific Ocean are among the best examples of shields. All of the Hawaiian volcanoes, for example, are basalt shield volcanoes, rising from the deep ocean to make the tallest mountains in the world.

Basalt-producing volcanoes are often connected to HOT SPOTS in the mantle or to places where the crust is pulling apart, such as OCEANIC RIDGES.

Where TECTONIC PLATES collide, the magma has a different composition and is less runny. As a result, it produces quite different landforms. Magma of this kind mainly occurs in newly forming mountain ranges.

*(Left and below)* Volcanoes that erupt lava can send out liquid rock that congeals on the earth's surface in thin sheets. This is new material from the mantle. Floods of lava may fill in old valleys and create new plains, thus creating new landforms. The Columbia-Snake plateau of the northwestern United States (bottom photograph) is a good example of a landscape changed by volcanic activity.

As magma rises into the cores of newly forming mountains, it melts and then incorporates many of the rocks around it. This magma contains more quartz and is far less runny. It also contains a large amount of material that, although quite liquid when under great pressure, becomes a gas when it reaches the surface. As a result, this material does not flow smoothly from volcanic vents but, instead, often explodes violently.

Explosive volcanoes produce a combination of ASH and LAVA. They are known as stratovolcanoes (because they are made of strata of ash and lava), composite volcanoes, or central vent volcanoes.

In the early stages of the eruption, while the pressure is still very high in the underground magma chamber, magma is blown out of the vent as ash. Later, when the pressure is less intense, it flows from the vent as lava. When the pressure is so low that it can no longer eject magma from the vent, the remaining material cools in the vent and forms a PLUG of lava. Lava plugs are large bodies of crystalline magma that is often much more resistant to erosion than the lava and ash that were ejected in the early stages of an eruption.

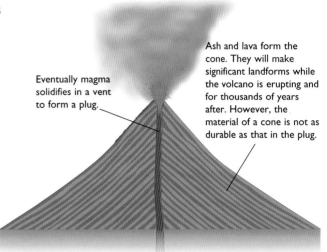

(Below) The structure of a STRATOVOLCANO.

Eventually magma solidifies in a vent to form a plug.

Ash and lava form the cone. They will make significant landforms while the volcano is erupting and for thousands of years after. However, the material of a cone is not as durable as that in the plug.

(Above and below) Agathla Peak, Arizona, USA, is a dramatic example of a volcanic plug. The outline below shows the possible position of the original volcano.

Original volcano

Dykes and sills

Plug

A volcano may have a life of thousands of years and may experience many eruptions, so that the cone builds layer on layer. Sometimes the pressure may be enough to force the magma to blow out of the side of the volcanic cone, so that new vents are formed. When these vents become quiet, the material in these side vents will also solidify as plugs of lava.

Volcanoes formed over magma chambers that are close to the surface may also collapse during a violent eruption. If this is the case, then the whole central part of the cone may fall inwards, creating a vast

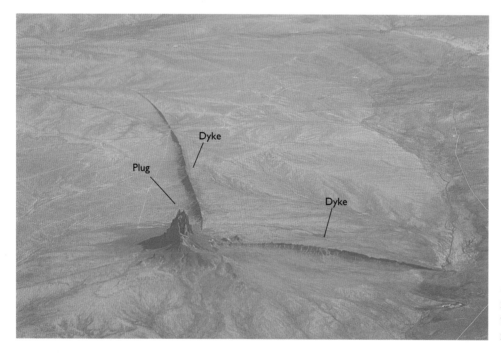

*(Left)* Ship Rock, New Mexico, USA, is a plug with radiating dykes.

*(Below)* Lava plugs make pillars of rock in the landscape. This is near Le Puy in France.

natural pit with just a ring of high land showing where the cone once was. Volcanoes with large central pits of this kind are called CALDERAS, and often they will fill with water to make CRATER LAKES.

Whatever the shape of the active volcano, when it eventually becomes extinct, erosion will strip away the soft ash from the slopes. The most resistant part of a stratovolcano, the plug and dykes that show where magma stretched out from the main vent to feeder vents, will often remain behind to show the location of the old vent.

*(Below)* The development of a crater lake by the formation of a caldera.

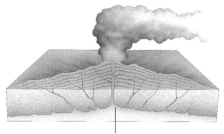

The volcano erupts violently so that the rocks are weakened. At the same time, the lava pours out of the vent so fast that the magma chamber is left partly empty.

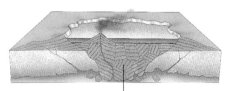

The weight of the volcano's cone makes it collapse in on the magma chamber, producing a vast pit that can then, over the following centuries, fill with water.

*(Left and below)* This is Crater Lake, Oregon, USA. You can see the caldera very clearly, since the flanks of the volcano are picked out by snow. Wizard Island is near the back of the lake on the aerial photograph.

Wizard Island

Dyke

(Left) Dykes cutting across horizontally bedded rocks in Big Bend National Park, Texas, USA.

Dyke

(Above) In this diagram the dyke is more resistant to weathering and erosion than the surrounding rock at the surface. As a result the dyke stands out.

(Below) A dyke on the Isle of Arran, Scotland. In this case the dyke is less resistant than the contact metamorphic rocks on either side, which were baked when the dyke was intruded. Since it has eroded more quickly, it has left a slot.

# Dykes

Dykes are walls of rock, which cut through older materials. Sometimes they reach the surface, and then magma flows out along a fissure.

While a dyke is being forced into the surrounding rocks, heat from the igneous rock will bake the rocks it touches This effect is called CONTACT METAMORPHISM, and rocks treated in this way become very hard, sometimes even harder and more resistant to erosion than the rocks of the dyke.

Dykes (and the baked rocks either side of them) are often more resistant to erosion than other kinds of rock and stand out in the landscape as long walls. In some places, there are very large numbers of dykes together. They are called DYKE SWARMS. They usually occur in places where, in the past, the crust has stretched as continents pulled apart. Such dykes can be hundreds of kilometres long. This is the case, for example, with the dyke swarms in Scotland, Northern Ireland, and northern England. They were formed at the time when the Atlantic Ocean was beginning to open up as a result of the slow westwards drift of North America from Europe.

Dyke

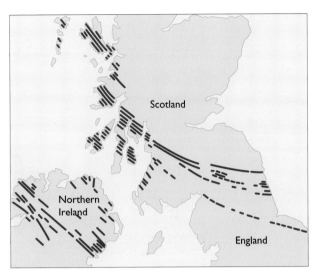

*(Left)* Dykes and sills in the northern British Isles.

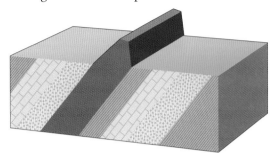

*(Below)* A sill may be seen as a ridge in the landscape.

# Sills

Sills are sheets of rock, which have a roof and a floor. That is, they have been injected between two existing layers of rock. As is the case with dykes, sills can bake the rocks they touch, making them also very hard and resistant to erosion. Sills are often formed at the same time as dykes.

Many sills form as thick bands of very resistant rock. They may make prominent ledges in a landscape. They are one of the rocks that commonly form the lip of a waterfall (see page 32).

# Batholiths

The volcanoes, dykes, and sills are all minor features compared with the magma chambers that were once the source of all other volcanic material. Only vast sheets of flood basalt have as great an impact on the landscape.

Magma chambers may be very large bodies of molten rock, feeding many volcanoes. It is the sheer size of the batholiths that provides the major impact on the landscape. Some batholiths are hundreds of kilometres long and many tens of kilometres wide. They are all formed of granite and are extremely resistant to erosion. They often form large, domed masses that mark the former cores of mountain ranges.

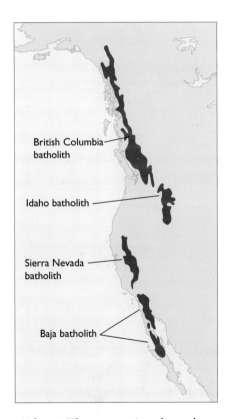

*(Above)* The mountains along the western coast of America contain huge, elongated batholiths. The picture on page 5 shows the landscape of Yosemite National Park, California, which is part of the Sierra Nevada batholith. Half Dome (see page 5) is a famous feature in the park and clearly shows the exposed granite batholith.

# Glossary

**aa lava:** a type of lava with a broken, bouldery surface.

**abrasion:** the rubbing away (erosion) of a rock by the physical scraping of particles carried by water, wind or ice.

**acidic rock:** a type of igneous rock that consists predominantly of light-coloured minerals and more than two-thirds silica (e.g. granite).

**active volcano:** a volcano that has observable signs of activity, for example, periodic plumes of steam.

**adit:** a horizontal tunnel drilled into rock.

**aftershock:** an earthquake that follows the main shock. Major earthquakes are followed by a number of aftershocks that decrease in frequency with time.

**agglomerate:** a rock made from the compacted particles thrown out by a volcano (e.g. tuff).

**alkaline rock:** a type of igneous rock containing less than half silica and normally dominated by dark-coloured minerals (e.g. gabbro).

**amygdule:** a vesicle in a volcanic rock filled with secondary minerals such as calcite, quartz or zeolite.

**andesite:** an igneous volcanic rock. Slightly more acidic than basalt.

**anticline:** an arching fold of rock layers in which the rocks slope down from the crest. *See also* syncline.

**Appalachian Mountain (Orogenic) Belt:** an old mountain range that extends for more than 3000 km along the eastern margin of North America from Alabama in the southern United States to Newfoundland, Canada, in the north. There were three Appalachian orogenies: Taconic (about 460 million years ago) in the Ordovician; Acadian (390 to 370 million years ago) in the Devonian; and Alleghenian (300 to 250 million years ago) in the Late Carboniferous to Permian. These mountain belts can be traced as the Caledonian and Hercynian orogenic belts in Europe.

**Archean Eon:** *see* eon.

**arenaceous:** a rock composed largely of sand grains.

**argillaceous:** a rock composed largely of clay.

**arkose:** a coarse sandstone formed by the disintegration of a granite.

**ash, volcanic:** fine powdery material thrown out of a volcano.

**asthenosphere:** the weak part of the upper mantle below the lithosphere, in which slow convection is thought to take place.

**augite:** a dark green-coloured silicate mineral containing calcium, sodium, iron, aluminium and magnesium.

**axis of symmetry:** a line or plane around which one part of a crystal is a mirror image of another part.

**basalt:** basic fine-grained igneous volcanic rock; lava often contains vesicles.

**basic rock:** an igneous rock (e.g. gabbro) with silica content less than two-thirds and containing a high percentage of dark-coloured minerals.

**basin:** a large, circular, or oval sunken region on the earth's surface created by downwards folding. A river basin, or watershed, is the area drained by a river and its tributaries.

**batholith:** a very large body of plutonic rock that was intruded deep into the earth's crust and is now exposed by erosion.

**bauxite:** a surface material that contains a high percentage of aluminium silicate. The principal ore of aluminium.

**bed:** a layer of sediment. It may involve many phases of deposition, each marked by a bedding plane.

**bedding plane:** an ancient surface on which sediment built up. Sedimentary rocks often split along bedding planes.

**biotite:** a black-coloured form of mica.

**body wave:** a seismic wave that can travel through the interior of the earth. P waves and S waves are body waves.

**boss:** an upwards extension of a batholith. A boss may once have been a magma chamber.

**botryoidal:** the shape of a mineral that resembles a bunch of grapes, e.g. haematite the crystals of which are often arranged in massive clumps, giving a surface covered with spherical bulges.

**butte:** a small mesa.

**calcareous:** composed mainly of calcium carbonate.

**calcite:** a mineral composed of calcium carbonate.

**caldera:** the collapsed cone of a volcano. It sometimes contains a crater lake.

**Caledonian Mountain-Building Period, Caledonian Orogeny:** a major mountain-building period in the Lower Paleozoic Era that reached its climax at the end of the Silurian Period (430 to 395 million years ago). An early phase affected only North America and made part of the Appalachian Mountain Belt.

**Cambrian, Cambrian Period:** the first period of geological time in the Paleozoic Era, beginning 570 million years ago and ending 500 million years ago.

**carbonate minerals:** minerals formed with carbonate ions (e.g. calcite).

**Carboniferous, Carboniferous Period:** a period of geological time between about 345 and 280 million years ago. It is often divided into the Early Carboniferous Epoch (345 to 320 million years ago) and the Late Carboniferous Epoch (320 to 280 million years ago). The Late Carboniferous is characterised by large coal-forming swamps. In North America the Carboniferous is usually divided into the Mississippian (= Lower Carboniferous) and Pennsylvanian (= Upper Carboniferous) periods.

**cast, fossil:** the natural filling of a mould by sediment or minerals that were left when a fossil dissolved after being enclosed by rock.

**Cenozoic, Cenozoic Era:** the most recent era of geological time, beginning 65 million years ago and continuing to the present.

**central vent volcano:** *see* stratovolcano.

**chemical compound:** a substance made from the chemical combination of two or more elements.

**chemical rock:** a rock produced by chemical precipitation (e.g. halite).

**chemical weathering:** the decay of a rock through the chemical action of water containing dissolved acidic gases.

**cinder cone:** a volcanic cone made entirely of cinders. Cinder cones have very steep sides.

**class:** the level of biological classification below a phylum.

**clast:** an individual grain of a rock.

**clastic rock:** a sedimentary rock that is made up of fragments of pre-existing rocks, carried by gravity, water, or wind (e.g. conglomerate, sandstone).

**cleavage:** the tendency of some minerals to break along one or more smooth surfaces.

**coal:** the carbon-rich, solid mineral derived from fossilised plant remains. Found in sedimentary rocks. Types of coal include bituminous, brown, lignite, and anthracite. A fossil fuel.

**complex volcano:** a volcano that has had an eruptive history and which produces two or more vents.

**composite volcano:** *see* stratovolcano.

**concordant coast:** a coast where the geological structure is parallel to the coastline. *See also* discordant coastline.

**conduction (of heat):** the transfer of heat between touching objects.

**conglomerate:** a coarse-grained sedimentary rock with grains larger than 2 mm.

**contact metamorphism:** metamorphism that occurs owing to direct contact with a molten magma. *See also* regional metamorphism.

**continental drift:** the theory suggested by Alfred Wegener that earth's continents were originally one land mass which split up to form the arrangement of continents we see today.

**continental shelf:** the ocean floor from the coastal shore of continents to the continental slope.

**continental shield:** the ancient and stable core of a tectonic plate. Also called a shield.

**convection:** the slow overturning of a liquid or gas that is heated from below.

**cordillera:** a long mountain belt consisting of many mountain ranges.

**core:** the innermost part of the earth. The earth's core is very dense, rich in iron, partly molten, and the source of the earth's magnetic field. The inner core is solid and has a radius of about 1300 kilometres. The outer core is fluid and is about 2100 kilometres thick. S waves cannot travel through the outer core.

**cracking:** the breaking up of a hydrocarbon compound into simpler constituents by means of heat.

**crater lake:** a lake found inside a caldera.

**craton:** *see* shield.

**Cretaceous, Cretaceous Period:** the third period of the Mesozoic Era. It lasted from about 135 to 65 million years ago. It was a time of chalk formation and when many dinosaurs lived.

**cross-bedding:** a pattern of deposits in a sedimentary rock in which many thin layers lie at an angle to the bedding planes, showing that the sediment was deposited by a moving fluid. Wind-deposited cross-beds are often bigger than water-deposited beds.

**crust:** the outermost layer of the earth, typically 5 km under the oceans and 50 to 100 km thick under continents. It makes up less than 1 per cent of the earth's volume.

**crustal plate:** *see* tectonic plate.

**crystal:** a mineral that has a regular geometric shape and is bounded by smooth, flat faces.

**crystal system:** a group of crystals with the same arrangement of axes.

**crystalline:** a mineral that has solidified but has been unable to produce well-formed crystals. Quartz and halite are commonly found as crystalline masses.

**crystallisation:** the formation of crystals.

**cubic:** a crystal system in which crystals have 3 axes all at right angles to one another and of equal length.

**cuesta:** a ridge in the landscape formed by a resistant band of dipping rock. A cuesta has a steep scarp slope and a more gentle dip slope.

**current bedding:** a pattern of deposits in a sedimentary rock in which many thin layers lie at an angle to the bedding planes, showing that the sediment was deposited by a current of water.

**cyclothem:** a repeating sequence of rocks found in coal strata.

**delta:** a triangle of deposition produced where a river enters a sea or lake.

**deposit, deposition:** the process of laying down material that has been transported in suspension or solution by water, ice, or wind. A deposit is the material laid down by deposition (e.g. salt deposits).

**destructive plate boundary:** a line where plates collide and where one plate is subducted into the mantle.

**Devonian, Devonian Period:** the fourth period of geological time in the Palaeozoic Era, from 395 to 345 million years ago.

**diorite:** an igneous plutonic rock between gabbro and granite; the plutonic equivalent of andesite.

**dip:** the angle that a bedding plane or fault makes with the horizontal.

**dip slope:** the more gently sloping part of a cuesta whose surface often parallels the dip of the strata.

**discontinuity:** a gap in deposition, perhaps caused by the area being lifted above the sea so that erosion, rather than deposition, occurred for a time.

**discordant coast:** a coast where the rock structure is at an angle to the line of the coast. *See also* concordant coastline.

**displacement:** the distance over which one piece of rock is pushed relative to another.

**dissolve:** to break down a substance into a solution without causing a reaction.

**distillation:** the boiling off of volatile materials, leaving a residue.

**dolomite:** a mineral composed of calcium magnesium carbonate.

**dome:** a circular, uplifted region of rocks taking the shape of a dome and found in some areas of folded rocks. Rising plugs of salt will also dome up the rocks above them. They sometimes make oil traps.

**dormant volcano:** a volcano that shows no signs of activity but which has been active in the recent past.

**drift:** a tunnel drilled in rock and designed to provide a sloping route for carrying out ore or coal by means of a conveyor belt.

**dyke:** a wall-like sheet of igneous rock that cuts across the layers of the surrounding rocks.

**dyke swarm:** a collection of hundreds or thousands of parallel dykes.

**earthquake:** shaking of the earth's surface caused by a sudden movement of rock within the earth.

**element:** a fundamental chemical building block. A substance that cannot be separated into simpler substances by any chemical means. Oxygen and sulphur are examples of elements.

**eon:** the largest division of geological time. An eon is subdivided into eras. Precambrian time is divided into the Archean (earlier than 2.5 billion years ago) and Proterozoic eons (more recent than 2.5 billion years ago). The Phanerozoic Eon includes the Cambrian Period to the present.

**epicentre:** the point on the earth's surface directly above the focus (hypocentre) of an earthquake.

**epoch:** a subdivision of a geological period in the geological time scale (e.g. Pleistocene Epoch).

**era:** a subdivision of a geological eon in the geological time scale (e.g. Cenozoic Era). An era is subdivided into periods.

**erode, erosion:** the twin processes of breaking down a rock (called weathering) and then removing the debris (called transporting).

**escarpment:** the crest of a ridge made of dipping rocks.

**essential mineral:** the dominant mineral constituents of a rock used to classify it.

**evaporite:** a mineral or rock formed as the result of evaporation of salt-laden water, such as a lagoon or salt lake.

**exoskeleton:** another word for shell. Applies to invertebrates.

**extinct volcano:** a volcano that has shown no signs of activity in historic times.

**extrusive rock, extrusion:** an igneous volcanic rock that has solidified on the surface of the earth.

**facet:** the cleaved face of a mineral. Used in describing jewellery.

**facies:** physical, chemical, or biological variations in a sedimentary bed of the same geological age (e.g. sandy facies, limestone facies).

**family:** a part of the classification of living things above a genus.

**fault:** a deep fracture or zone of fractures in rocks along which there has been displacement of one side relative to the other. It represents a weak point in the crust and upper mantle.

**fault scarp:** a long, straight, steep slope in the landscape that has been produced by faulting.

**feldspar:** the most common silicate mineral. It consists of two forms: plagioclase and orthoclase.

**ferromagnesian mineral:** dark-coloured minerals, such as augite and hornblende, which contain relatively high proportions of iron and magnesium and low proportions of silica.

**fissure:** a substantial crack in a rock.

**fjord:** a glaciated valley in a mountainous area coastal area that has been partly flooded by the sea.

**focal depth:** the depth of an earthquake focus below the surface.

**focus:** the origin of an earthquake, directly below the epicentre.

**fold:** arched or curved rock strata.

**fold axis:** line following the highest arching in an anticline, or the lowest arching in a syncline.

**fold belt:** a part of a mountain system containing folded sedimentary rocks.

**foliation:** a texture of a rock (usually schist) that resembles the pages in a book.

**formation:** a word used to describe a collection of related rock layers or beds. A number of related beds make a member; a collection of related members makes up a formation. Formations are often given location names, e.g. Toroweap Formation, the members of which are a collection of dominantly limestone beds.

**fossil:** any evidence of past life, including remains, traces and imprints.

**fossil fuel:** any fuel that was formed in the geological past from the remains of living organisms. The main fossil fuels are coal and petroleum (oil and natural gas).

**fraction:** one of the components of crude oil that can be separated from others by heating and then by cooling the vapour.

**fracture:** a substantial break across a rock.

**fracture zone:** a region in which fractures are common. Fracture zones are particularly common in folded rock and near faults.

**frost shattering:** the process of breaking pieces of rock through the action of freezing and melting of rainwater

**gabbro:** alkaline igneous plutonic rock, typically showing dark-coloured crystals; plutonic equivalent of basalt.

**gallery:** a horizontal access tunnel in a mine.

**gangue:** the unwanted mineral matter found in association with a metal.

**gem:** a mineral, usually in crystal form, that is regarded as having particular beauty and value.

**genus:** (*pl.* genera) the biological classification for a group of closely related species.

**geode:** a hollow lump of rock (nodule) that often contains crystals.

**geological column:** a columnar diagram showing the divisions of geological time (eons, eras, periods, and epochs).

**geological eon:** *see* eon.

**geological epoch:** *see* epoch.

**geological era:** *see* era.

**geological period:** a subdivision of a geological era (e.g. Carboniferous Period). A period is subdivided into epochs.

**geological system:** a term for an accumulation of strata that occurs during a geological period (e.g. the Ordovician System is the rocks deposited during the Ordovician Period). Systems are divided into series.

**geological time:** the history of the earth revealed by its rocks.

**geological time scale:** the division of geological time into eons, era, periods, and epochs.

**geosyncline:** a large, slowly subsiding region marginal to a continent where huge amounts of sediment accumulate. The rocks in a geosyncline are eventually lifted to form mountain belts.

**gneiss:** a metamorphic rock showing large grains.

**graben:** a fallen block of the earth's crust forming a long trough, separated on all sides by faults. Associated with rift valleys.

**grain:** a particle of a rock or mineral.

**granite:** an acidic, igneous, plutonic rock containing free quartz, typically light in colour; plutonic equivalent of rhyolite.

**grit:** grains larger than sand but smaller than stones.

**groundmass:** *see* matrix.

**group:** a word used to describe a collection of related rock layers, or beds. A number of related beds make a member; a collection of related members makes up a formation; a collection of related formations makes a group.

**gypsum:** a mineral made of calcium sulphate.

**halide minerals:** a group of minerals (e.g. halite) that contain a halogen element (elements similar to chlorine) bonded with another element. Many are evaporite minerals.

**halite:** a mineral made of sodium chloride.

**Hawaiian-type eruption:** a name for a volcanic eruption that mainly consists of lava fountains.

**hexagonal:** a crystal system in which crystals have 3 axes all at 120 degrees to one another and of equal length.

**hogback:** a cuesta where the scarp and dip slopes are at about the same angle.

**hornblende:** a dark-green silicate mineral of the amphibole group containing sodium, potassium, calcium, magnesium, iron and aluminium.

**horst:** a raised block of the earth's crust separated on all sides by faults. Associated with rift valleys.

**hot spot:** a place where a fixed mantle magma plume reaches the surface.

**hydraulic action:** the erosive action of water pressure on rocks.

**hydrothermal:** a change brought about in a rock or mineral due to the action of superheated mineral-rich fluids, usually water.

**hypocentre:** the calculated location of the focus of an earthquake.

**ice wedging:** *see* frost shattering.

**Icelandic-type eruption:** a name given to a fissure type of eruption.

**igneous rock:** rock formed by the solidification of magma. Igneous rocks include volcanic and plutonic rocks.

**impermeable:** a rock that will not allow a liquid to pass through it.

**imprint:** a cast left by a former life form.

**impurities:** small amounts of elements or compounds in an otherwise homogeneous mineral.

**index fossil:** a fossil used as a marker for a particular part of geological time.

**intrusive rock, intrusion:** rocks that have formed from cooling magma below the surface. When inserted amongst other rocks, intruded rocks are called an intrusion.

**invertebrate:** an animal with an external skeleton.

**ion:** a charged particle.

**island arc:** a pattern of volcanic islands that follows the shape of an arc when seen from above.

**isostacy:** the principle that a body can float in a more dense fluid. The same as buoyancy, but used for continents.

**joint:** a significant crack between blocks of rock, normally used in the context of patterns of cracks.

**Jurassic, Jurassic Period:** the second geological period in the Mesozoic Era, lasting from about 190 to 135 million years ago.

**kingdom:** the broadest division in the biological classification of living things.

**laccolith:** a lens-shaped body of intrusive igneous rock with a dome-shaped upper surface and a flat bottom surface.

**landform:** a recognisable shape of part of the landscape, for example, a cuesta.

**landslide:** the rapid movement of a slab of soil down a steep hillslope.

**lateral fault:** *see* thrust fault.

**laterite:** a surface deposit containing a high proportion of iron.

**lava:** molten rock material extruded onto the surface of the earth.

**lava bomb:** *see* volcanic bomb.

**law of superposition:** the principle that younger rock is deposited on older.

**limestone:** a carbonate sedimentary rock composed of more than half calcium carbonate.

**lithosphere:** that part of the crust and upper mantle which is brittle and makes up the tectonic plates.

**lode:** a mining term for a rock containing many rich ore-bearing minerals. Similar to vein.

**Love wave, L wave:** a major type of surface earthquake wave that shakes the ground surface at right angles to the direction in which the wave is travelling. It is named after A.E.H. Love, the English mathematician who discovered it.

**lustre:** the way in which a mineral reflects light. Used as a test when identifying minerals.

**magma:** the molten material that comes from the mantle and which cools to form igneous rocks.

**magma chamber:** a large cavity melted in the earth's crust and filled with magma. Many magma chambers are plumes of magma that have melted their way from the mantle to the upper part of the crust. When a magma chamber is no longer supplied with molten magma, the magma solidifies to form a granite batholith.

**mantle:** the layer of the earth between the crust and the core. It is approximately 2900 kilometres thick and is the largest of the earth's major layers.

**marginal accretion:** the growth of mountain belts on the edges of a shield.

**mass extinction:** a time when the majority of species on the planet were killed off.

**matrix:** the rock or sediment in which a fossil is embedded; the fine-grained rock in which larger particles are embedded, for example, in a conglomerate.

**mechanical weathering:** the disintegration of a rock by frost shattering/ice wedging.

**mesa:** a large detached piece of a tableland.

**Mesozoic, Mesozoic Era:** the geological era between the Palaeozoic and the Cenozoic eras. It lasted from about 225 to 65 million years ago.

**metamorphic aureole:** the region of contact metamorphic rock that surrounds a batholith.

**metamorphic rock:** any rock (e.g. schist, gneiss) that was formed from a pre-existing rock by heat and pressure.

**meteorite:** a substantial chunk of rock in space.

**micas:** a group of soft, sheet-like silicate minerals (e.g. biotite, muscovite).

**mid-ocean ridge:** a long mountain chain on the ocean floor where basalt periodically erupts, forming new oceanic crust.

**mineral:** a naturally occurring inorganic substance of definite chemical composition (e.g. calcite, calcium carbonate).
More generally, any resource extracted from the ground by mining (includes metal ores, coal, oil, gas, rocks, etc.).

**mineral environment:** the place where a mineral or a group of associated minerals form. Mineral environments include igneous, sedimentary, and metamorphic rocks.

**mineralisation:** the formation of minerals within a rock.

**Modified Mercalli Scale:** a scale for measuring the impact of an earthquake. It is composed of 12 increasing levels of intensity, which range from imperceptible, designated by Roman numeral I, to catastrophic destruction, designated by XII.

**Mohorovicic discontinuity:** the boundary surface that separates the earth's crust from the underlying mantle. Named after Andrija Mohorovicic, a Croatian seismologist.

**Mohs' Scale of Hardness:** a relative scale developed to put minerals into an order. The hardest is 10 (diamond), and the softest is 1 (talc).

**monoclinic:** a crystal system in which crystals have 2 axes all at right angles to one another, and each axis is of unequal length.

**mould:** an impression in a rock of the outside of an organism.

**mountain belt:** a region where there are many ranges of mountains. The term is often applied to a wide belt of mountains produced during mountain building.

**mountain building:** the creation of mountains as a result of the collision of tectonic plates. Long belts or chains of mountains can form along the edge of a continent during this process. Mountain building is also called orogeny.

**mountain building period:** a period during which a geosyncline is compressed into fold mountains by the collision of two tectonic plates. Also known as orogenesis.

**mudstone:** a fine-grained, massive rock formed by the compaction of mud.

**nappe:** a piece of a fold that has become detached from its roots during intensive mountain building.

**native metal:** a metal that occurs uncombined with any other element.

**natural gas:** *see* petroleum.

**normal fault:** a fault in which one block has slipped down the face of another. It is the most common kind of fault and results from tension.

**nueé ardente:** another word for pyroclastic flow.

**ocean trench:** a deep, steep-sided trough in the ocean floor caused by the subduction of oceanic crust beneath either other oceanic crust or continental crust.

**olivine:** the name of a group of magnesium iron silicate minerals that have an olive colour.

**order:** a level of biological classification between class and family.

**Ordovician, Ordovician Period:** the second period of geological time within the Palaeozoic Era. It lasted from about 500 to 430 million years ago.

**ore:** a rock containing enough useful metal or fuel to be worth mining.

**ore mineral:** a mineral that occurs in sufficient quantity to be mined for its metal. The compound must also be easy to process.

**organic rocks:** rocks formed by living things, for example, coal.

**orthoclase:** the form of feldspar that is often pink in colour and which contains potassium as important ions.

**orogenic belt:** a mountain belt.

**orogeny:** a period of mountain building. Orogenesis is the process of mountain building and the creation of orogenic belts.

**orthorhombic:** a crystal system in which crystals have 3 axes all at right angles to one another but of unequal length.

**outcrop:** the exposure of a rock at the surface of the earth.

**overburden:** the unwanted layer(s) of rock above an ore or coal body.

**oxide minerals:** a group of minerals in which oxygen is a major constituent. A compound in which oxygen is bonded to another element or group.

**Pacific Ring of Fire:** the ring of volcanoes and volcanic activity that circles the Pacific Ocean. Created by the collision of the Pacific Plate with its neighbouring plates.

**pahoehoe lava:** the name for a form of lava that has a smooth surface.

**Palaeozoic, Palaeozoic Era:** a major interval of geological time. The Palaeozoic is the oldest era in which fossil life is commonly found. It lasted from about 570 to 225 million years ago.

**palaeomagnetism:** the natural magnetic traces that reveal the intensity and direction of the earth's magnetic field in the geological past.

**pegmatite:** an igneous rock (e.g. a dyke) of extremely coarse crystals.

**Pelean-type eruption:** a violent explosion dominated by pyroclastic flows.

**period:** *see* geological period.

**permeable rock:** a rock that will allow a fluid to pass through it.

**Permian, Permian Period:** the last period of the Palaeozoic Era, lasting from about 280 to 225 million years ago.

**petrified:** when the tissues of a dead plant or animal have been replaced by minerals, such as silica, they are said to be petrified (e.g. petrified wood).

**petrified forest:** a large number of fossil trees. Most petrified trees are replaced by silica.

**petroleum:** the carbon-rich, and mostly liquid, mixture produced by the burial and partial alteration of animal and plant remains. Petroleum is found in many sedimentary rocks. The liquid part of petroleum is called oil, the gaseous part is known as natural gas. Petroleum is an important fossil fuel.

**petroleum field:** a region from which petroleum can be recovered.

**Phanerozoic Eon:** the most recent eon, beginning at the Cambrian Period, some 570 million years ago, and extending up to the present.

**phenocryst:** an especially large crystal (in a porphyritic rock), embedded in smaller mineral grains.

**phylum:** (*pl.* phyla) biological classification for one of the major divisions of animal life and second in complexity to kingdom. The plant kingdom is not divided into phyla but into divisions.

**placer deposit:** a sediment containing heavy metal grains (e.g. gold) that have weathered out of the bedrock and are concentrated on a stream bed or along a coast.

**plagioclase:** the form of feldspar that is often white or grey and which contains sodium and calcium as important ions.

**planetismals:** small embryo planets.

**plate:** *see* tectonic plate.

**plateau:** an extensive area of raised flat land. The cliff-like edges of a plateau may, when eroded, leave isolated features such as mesas and buttes. *See also* tableland.

**plate tectonics:** the theory that the earth's crust and upper mantle (the lithosphere) are broken into a number of more or less rigid, but constantly moving, slabs or plates.

**Plinian-type eruption:** an explosive eruption that sends a column of ash high into the air.

**plug:** *see* volcanic plug

**plunging fold:** a fold whose axis dips, or plunges, into the ground.

**plutonic rock:** an igneous rock that has solidified at great depth and contains large crystals due to the slowness of cooling (e.g. granite, gabbro).

**porphyry, porphyritic rock:** an igneous rock in which larger crystals (phenocrysts) are enclosed in a fine-grained matrix.

**Precambrian, Precambrian time:** the whole of earth history before the Cambrian Period. Also called Precambrian Era and Precambrian Eon.

**precipitate:** a substance that has settled out of a liquid as a result of a chemical reaction between two chemicals in the liquid.

**Primary Era:** an older name for the Palaeozoic Era.

**prismatic:** a word used to describe a mineral that has formed with one axis very much longer than the others.

**Proterozoic Eon:** *see* eon.

**P wave, primary wave, primary seismic wave:** P waves are the fastest body waves. The waves carry energy in the same line as the direction of the wave. P waves can travel through all layers of the earth and are generally felt as a thump. *See also* S wave.

**pyrite:** iron sulphide. It is common in sedimentary rocks that were poor in oxygen, and sometimes forms fossil casts.

**pyroclastic flow:** solid material ejected from a volcano, combined with searingly hot gases, which together behave as a high-density fluid. Pyroclastic flows can do immense damage, as was the case with Mount Saint Helens.

**pyroclastic material:** any solid material ejected from a volcano.

**Quaternary, Quaternary Period:** the second period in the Cenozoic Era, beginning about 1.6 million years ago and continuing to the present day.

**radiation:** the transfer of energy between objects that are not in contact.

**radioactive dating:** the dating of a material by the use of its radioactive elements. The rate of decay of any element changes in a predictable way, allowing a precise date to be given of when the material was formed.

**rank:** a name used to describe the grade of coal in terms of its possible heat output. The higher the rank, the more the heat output.

**Rayleigh wave:** a type of surface wave having an elliptical motion similar to the waves caused when a stone is dropped into a pond. It is the slowest, but often the largest and most destructive, of the wave types caused by an earthquake. It is usually felt as a rolling or rocking motion and, in the case of major earthquakes, can be seen as they approach. Named after Lord Rayleigh, the English physicist who predicted its existence.

**regional metamorphism:** metamorphism resulting from both heat and pressure. It is usually connected with mountain building and occurs over a large area. *See also* contact metamorphism.

**reniform:** a kidney-shaped mineral habit (e.g. hematite).

**reservoir rock:** a permeable rock in which petroleum accumulates.

**reversed fault:** a fault where one slab of the earth's crust rides up over another. Reversed faults are only common during plate collision.

**rhyolite:** acid, igneous, volcanic rock, typically light in colour; volcanic equivalent of granite.

**ria:** the name for a partly flooded coastal river valley in an area where the landscape is hilly.

**Richter Scale:** the system used to measure the strength of an earthquake. Developed by Charles Richter, an American, in 1935.

**rift, rift valley:** long troughs on continents and mid-ocean ridges that are bounded by normal faults.

**rifting:** the process of crustal stretching that causes blocks of crust to subside, creating rift valleys.

**rock:** a naturally occurring solid material containing one or more minerals.

**rock cycle:** the continuous sequence of events that cause mountains to be formed, then eroded, before being formed again.

**rupture:** the place over which an earthquake causes rocks to move against one another.

**salt dome:** a balloon-shaped mass of salt produced by salt being forced upwards under pressure.

**sandstone:** a sedimentary rock composed of cemented sand-sized grains 0.06–2 mm in diameter.

**scarp slope:** the steep slope of a cuesta.

**schist:** a metamorphic rock characterised by a shiny surface of mica crystals all orientated in the same direction.

**scoria:** the rough, often foam-like rock that forms on the surface of some lavas.

**seamount:** a volcano that rises from the sea bed.

**Secondary Era:** an older term for a geological era. Now replaced by Mesozoic Era.

**sediment:** any solid material that has settled out of suspension in a liquid.

**sedimentary rock:** a layered clastic rock formed through the deposition of pieces of mineral, rock, animal or vegetable matter.

**segregation:** the separation of minerals.

**seismic gap:** a part of an active fault where there have been no earthquakes in recent times.

**seismic wave:** a wave generated by an earthquake.

**series:** the rock layers that correspond to an epoch of time.

**shadow zone:** the region of the earth that experiences no shocks after an earthquake.

**shaft:** a vertical tunnel that provides access or ventilation to a mine.

**shale:** a fine-grained sedimentary rock made of clay minerals with particle sizes smaller than 2 microns.

**shield:** the ancient and stable core of a tectonic plate. Also called a continental shield.

**shield volcano:** a volcano with a broad, low-angled cone made entirely of lava.

**silica, silicate:** silica is silicon dioxide. It is a very common mineral, occurring as quartz, chalcedony, etc. A silicate is any mineral that contains silica.

**sill:** a tabular, sheet-like body of intrusive igneous rock that has been injected between layers of sedimentary or metamorphic rock.

**Silurian, Silurian Period:** the name of the third geological period of the Palaeozoic Era. It began about 430 and ended about 395 million years ago.

**skarn:** a mineral deposit formed by the chemical reaction of hot acidic fluids and carbonate rocks.

**slag:** waste rock material that becomes separated from the metal during smelting.

**slate:** a low-grade metamorphic rock produced by pressure, in which the clay minerals have arranged themselves parallel to one another.

**slaty cleavage:** a characteristic pattern found in slates in which the parallel arrangement of clay minerals causes the rock to fracture (cleave) in sheets.

**species:** a population of animals or plants capable of interbreeding.

**spreading boundary:** a line where two plates are being pulled away from each other. New crust is formed as molten rock is forced upwards into the gap.

**stock:** a vertical protrusion of a batholith that pushes up closer to the surface.

**stratigraphy:** the study of the earth's rocks in the context of their history and conditions of formation.

**stratovolcano:** a tall volcanic mountain made of alternating layers, or strata, of ash and lava.

**stratum:** (*pl.* strata) a layer of sedimentary rock.

**streak:** the colour of the powder of a mineral produced by rubbing the mineral against a piece of unglazed, white porcelain. Used as a test when identifying minerals.

**striation:** minute parallel grooves on crystal faces.

**strike, direction of:** the direction of a bedding plane or fault at right angles to the dip.

**Strombolian-type eruption:** a kind of volcanic eruption that is explosive enough

to send out some volcanic bombs.

**subduction:** the process of one tectonic plate descending beneath another.

**subduction zone:** the part of the earth's surface along which one tectonic plate descends into the mantle. It is often shaped in the form of an number of arcs.

**sulphides:** a group of important ore minerals (e.g. pyrite, galena, and sphalerite) in which sulphur combines with one or more metals.

**surface wave:** any one of a number of waves such as Love waves or Rayleigh waves that shake the ground surface just after an earthquake. *See also* Love waves and Rayleigh waves.

**suture:** the junction of 2 or more parts of a skeleton; in cephalopods the junction of a septum with the inner surface of the shell wall. It is very distinctive in ammonoids and used to identify them.

**S wave, shear or secondary seismic wave:** this kind of wave carries energy through the earth like a rope being shaken. S waves cannot travel through the outer core of the earth because they cannot pass through fluids. *See also* P wave.

**syncline:** a downfold of rock layers in which the rocks slope up from the bottom of the fold. *See also* anticline.

**system:** *see* geological system.

**tableland:** another word for a plateau. *See* plateau.

**tectonic plate:** one of the great slabs, or plates, of the lithosphere (the earth's crust and part of the earth's upper mantle) that covers the whole of the earth's surface. The earth's plates are separated by zones of volcanic and earthquake activity.

**Tertiary, Tertiary Period:** the first period of the Cenozoic Era. It began 665 and ended about 1.6 million years ago.

**thrust fault:** *see* reversed fault.

**transcurrent fault:** *see* lateral fault.

**transform fault:** *see* lateral fault.

**translucent:** a description of a mineral that allows light to penetrate but not pass through.

**transparent:** a description of a mineral that allows light to pass right through.

**trellis drainage pattern:** a river drainage system where the trunk river and its tributaries tend to meet at right angles.

**trench:** *see* ocean trench.

**Triassic, Triassic Period:** the first period of the Mesozoic era. It lasted from about 225 to 190 million years ago.

**triclinic:** a crystal system in which crystals have 3 axes, none at right angles or of equal length to one another.

**tsunami:** a very large wave produced by an underwater earthquake.

**tuff:** a rock made from volcanic ash.

**unconformity:** any interruption in the depositional sequence of sedimentary rocks.

**valve:** in bivalves and brachiopods, one of the separate parts of the shell.

**vein:** a sheet-like body of mineral matter (e.g. quartz) that cuts across a rock. Veins are often important sources of valuable minerals. Miners call such important veins lodes.

**vent:** the vertical pipe that allows the passage of magma through the centre of a volcano.

**vertebrate:** an animal with an internal skeleton.

**vesicle:** a small cavity in a volcanic rock originally created by an air bubble trapped in the molten lava.

**viscous, viscosity:** sticky, stickiness.

**volatile:** substances that tend to evaporate or boil off of a liquid.

**volcanic:** anything from, or of, a volcano. Volcanic rocks are igneous rocks that cool as they are released at the earth's surface – including those formed underwater; typically have small crystals due to the rapid cooling, e.g. basalt, andesite and rhyolite.

**volcanic bomb:** a large piece of magma thrown out of a crater during an eruption, which solidifies as it travels through cool air.

**volcanic eruption:** an ejection of ash or lava from a volcano.

**volcanic glass:** lava that has solidified very quickly and has not had time to develop any crystals. Obsidian is a volcanic glass.

**volcanic plug:** the solidified core of an extinct volcano.

**Vulcanian-type eruption:** an explosive form of eruption without a tall ash column or pyroclastic flow.

**water gap:** a gap cut by a superimposed river, which is still occupied by the river.

**weather, weathered, weathering:** the process of weathering is the mechanical action of ice and the chemical action of rainwater on rock, breaking it down into small pieces that can then be carried away. *See also* chemical weathering and mechanical weathering.

**wind gap:** a gap cut by a superimposed river, which is no longer occupied by the river.

# Set Index

## USING THE SET INDEX

This index covers all eight volumes in the *Earth Science* set:

Volume
number          Title

1:      Minerals
2:      Rocks
3:      Fossils
4:      Earthquakes and volcanoes
5:      Plate tectonics
6:      Landforms
7:      Geological time
8:      The earth's resources

An example entry:

Index entries are
listed alphabetically.

plagioclase feldspar **1:** *51*; **2:** 10 *see also*
feldspars

Volume numbers are in bold and are
followed by page references. Articles on a
subject are shown by italic page numbers.
In the example above, 'plagioclase
feldspar' appears in Volume 1: Minerals on
page 51 as a full article and in Volume 2:
Rocks on page 10. Many terms also are
covered in the GLOSSARY on pages 60–65.
The *see also* refers to another entry
where there will be additional relevant
information.

## A

aa lava **2:** 24; **4:** 37, 44
abrasion **6:** 41
Aconcagua, Mount (Argentina) **5:** 38
Adirondacks, Adirondack Mountains (New
York) **7:** 27
adit **8:** 39, 46
African Plate **5:** 11, 50
African Shield **5:** 54, 55, 56
aftershocks **4:** 14, 15
agate **1:** *50*
Agathla Peak (Arizona) **6:** 55
agglomerate **2:** 18
Agricola **1:** 30
Alaska **5:** 35
    1964 earthquake **4:** 9, 10, 12, *22–25*
    oil fields **8:** 37
*Alethopteris* **3:** 49
Aleutian Islands (Alaska) **5:** 34, 35
algae **3:** 48, 51
Alleghenian Mountain Building Period **7:** 41
almandine garnet **1:** 52
Alps **5:** 44, 45–51; **7:** 54, 56

aluminium **1:** 7; **8:** 8, 11, 33
    ores **8:** *12*
amber, fossils in **3:** 10, 38, 59
amethyst **1:** 5, *48*, 49
ammonites **3:** 4, 15, 16, 24, *26–28*, 56, 58, 59
    recognising fossils **3:** 27
ammonoids **3:** *26–28*, 54, 55, 56, 57, 58
Ampato (Peru) **5:** 37
amphibians **3:** 42, 46, 54, 55, 56
amphiboles **1:** *56*; **2:** 12
amygdules **2:** 16
Anchorage (Alaska) **4:** 22, 23, 25
andalusite **1:** *52*
Andes Mountains, Andes (South America)
    **5:** 11, *36–38*
andesite **2:** 16, 18, 21, *23*; **4:** 38, 39
Angara Shield **5:** 57
anhydrite **1:** *46*
*Annularia* **3:** 49
Antarctic Plate **5:** 11
Antarctica **5:** 45
anthracite **8:** 28, 29
anticlines **6:** 37, 38, 39; **8:** 32
antimony **8:** 10
apatite **1:** 23, *47*
apophylite **1:** 24
Appalachian Mountain Belt **5:** 45
Appalachian Mountains, Appalachians
    (United States) **5:** 44, 45; **6:** 36, 37, 38,
    39, 40; **7:** 29, 30, 41, 53
    coal fields **8:** 35
aquamarine **1:** 25, *55*
Arabian Plate **5:** 11
aragonite **1:** 28, *44*
*Archaeopteryx* **3:** 58
Archean Eon **7:** 25
Arches National Park (Utah) **6:** 20
arches, coastal **6:** 41–46
archosaurs **3:** 57
Arduino, Giovanni **7:** 15
arenaceous rocks **2:** 42
argillaceous sandstone **2:** 43
arkose sandstone **2:** 42, 44
arsenic **1:** 31; **8:** 10, 45, 57
arthropods (Arthropoda) **3:** *38–41*, 51, 53, 54
*Articulatean* **3:** 48
Arun River (Nepal) **6:** 10
ash, volcanic **2:** 16, 18, 19; **4:** 35, 36; **6:** 24, 55
asthenosphere **5:** 6, 8, 9
Atlantic Ocean **5:** 23, 25; **7:** 50, 55, 57
    oil fields **8:** 37
*Atlantis*, research ship **5:** 25
Atlas Mountains (Morocco) **7:** 54
atmosphere, formation **7:** 24–27
augen gneiss **2:** 59
augite **1:** 7, 14, 16, *56*; **2:** 12
Australian Shield **5:** 54, 56, 57
Ayers Rock (Australia) **5:** 57
azurite **1:** 20, *44*

## B

Baltic Shield **5:** 57; **7:** 25
Baltica **7:** 30, 32, 34, 36, 39
banded gneiss **2:** 59
barite **1:** 27, *46*
basalt **1:** 12; **2:** 14, 15, 17, 20, 21, *23–25*; **4:** 37,
    38, 39, 42, 44, 46, 47, 48, 49; **5:** 25;
    **6:** 53, 54; **8:** 8

basalt columns **2:** 15, 25; **6:** 18, 26
Basin and Range **4:** 27, 28; **5:** 42; **6:** 49
basins **6:** 40
batholiths **1:** 11; **6:** 19, 52, 53, 59
    ore minerals **8:** 24
Bauer, Georg **1:** 30
bauxite **1:** *39*; **8:** *12*, 33, 41
bedding, bedding planes **2:** 32, 36, 37; **6:** 20,
    32
belemnites (Belemnoids) **3:** 4, *24–25*, 57, 58,
    59
    recognising fossils **3:** 24
Bendigo (Australia) **7:** 35; **8:** 43
*Bennetitalean* **3:** 48
beryl **1:** 27, *55*
Berzelius, Jons **1:** 30
Big Bend National Park (Texas) **5:** 13; **6:** 58
biotite **1:** *58*; **2:** 11 *see also* mica
birds **3:** 42, 57, 58
bismuth **1:** 31; **8:** 10
bituminous coal **8:** 28, 29, *36(map)*
bivalves (Bivalvia) **3:** *29–31*, 52, 56
    recognising fossils **3:** 30
bloodstone **1:** 50
Blue Ridge Mountains (United States) **5:** 45
body waves **4:** *8 see also* P and S waves
bony fish **3:** 44, 54
Bora Bora (French Polynesia) **4:** 43
borate minerals **1:** *45*
borax **1:** *45*; **8:** 27
bornite **1:** *36*; **8:** *15*
boss **6:** 52, 53
brachiopods (Brachiopoda) **3:** *21–23*, 52, 53,
    54, 55, 56
    recognising **3:** 21
Brazilian Shield **5:** 56
breccia **2:** *40–41*
Bristol Lake (California) **8:** 27
brittle stars **3:** 36
Broken Hill (Australia) **8:** *25*
brown coal *see* lignite
Bryce Canyon (Utah) **6:** 21; **7:** 5, 10, 13
Bushveld Complex (South Africa) **8:** 21
buttes **6:** 26, 27, 34

## C

Cabot Fault (Canada) **6:** 50
cadmium **8:** 11
calcareous skeleton **3:** 6
calcite **1:** 18, 19, 23, *44*; **2:** 13
calderas **4:** *58–59*; **5:** 23; **6:** 52, 57
Caledonian Mountain Building Period **7:** 35
Caledonian Mountains **5:** 45; **7:** 30, 35, 37, 38
California Valley **5:** 39
*Calymene* **3:** 41, 54
calyx **3:** 34, 35
Cambrian, Cambrian Period **3:** 50*(chart)*;
    **7:** 18*(name)*, 21*(chart)*, *32(map)–33*
    fossils **7:** 52
    life **7:** 33
    rocks **7:** 33
Canadian Rockies **5:** 40, 41 *see also* Rockies
Canadian Shield **5:** 56; **7:** 25, 27
Canyon del Colca (Peru) **5:** 37
canyons **6:** 26, 27
cap rocks **6:** 26–27, 30, 32, 53; **8:** 32
carbon **1:** 31
carbonate minerals **1:** *44–45*; **8:** 11, 53

Carboniferous, Carboniferous Period **3:** 50(*chart*); **7:** 18(*name*), 21(*chart*), 40(*map*)–41; **8:** 30, 35, 37
    fossils **3:** 55
    life **7:** 41
    plants **3:** 48, 49, 55
    rocks **7:** 41
Caribbean Plate **5:** 11, 38
carnelian **1:** 50
cartilaginous fish **3:** 45 *see also* sharks
Cascades, Cascade Range (United States/ Canada) **4:** 42, 52; **5:** 35, 39; **7:** 53, 56
cassiterite **1:** 40; **8:** *18*
cast, fossil **3:** 9, 10, 40
cat's eye **1:** 50
caves, coastal **6:** 41–46
    limestone **6:** 25
Cenozoic, Cenozoic Era **3:** 50 (*incl. chart*); **7:** 15(*name*), 21(*chart*), 53–54
    fossils **3:** 59
    life **7:** 53
centipedes **3:** 38
cephalopods **3:** *24–28*, 52
ceratites **3:** 26
cerussite **8:** 17
chain silicate minerals **1:** *56–57*
chalcedony **1:** *50*
chalcopyrite **1:** 21, *36*; **8:** 10, *15*, 18
chalk **6:** 45; **7:** 50, 51, 52
Cheddar Gorge (England) **7:** 40
chemical rocks **2:** 32
Chiltern Hills (England) **6:** 34
China **7:** 30, 32, 34, 36, 40, 42, 46
Chinese Shield **5:** 57
Chiricahua National Monument (Arizona) **6:** 24
chlorite **1:** 16, *58*; **2:** 58
chromate minerals **1:** *46*
chromite **1:** *39*; **8:** *12*, 21
chromium **8:** 11
    ores **8:** *12*
chrysocolla **8:** *13*
chrysotile **1:** 59
*Cidaris* **3:** *37*, 56
cinder cones **4:** 44; **6:** 52
cinders **2:** 18; **4:** 35
cirripede **3:** 38
citrine **1:** 20, *48*, 49
clams **3:** 29 *see* bivalves
classes (biol. classification) **3:** 16
clastic limestone **2:** 49
clastic rocks **2:** 32
clasts **2:** 40
clay minerals **1:** 17, 19; **2:** 13
    mining **8:** 7
*Climacograptus* **3:** 43
Climax Mine (Colorado) **1:** 35; **8:** 8, 25
Clinton Formation **8:** 27
coal **2:** *49–51*; **3:** 55, 57; **5:** 16; **7:** 40, 41, 47, 51, 51; **8:** 5, 7, 35–36, 38, 41
    formation **8:** *28–30*
    location **8:** *35–36*
    rank **8:** 28
Coal Measures **7:** 40
Coast Ranges (United States) **5:** 39
coastal landforms **6:** 41–46
cobalt **8:** 10
coccoliths **7:** 50, 51

coke **8:** 55, 56, 57
collision plate boundaries **5:** 28, *32–51*, continent-continent collisions **5:** *43–51* ocean-continent collisions **5:** *36–42* ocean-ocean collisions **5:** *34–35*
Cologne (Germany), coal fields **8:** 36
Colorado Plateau (United States) **5:** 39, 41; **6:** 26
Columbia-Snake region (United States) **5:** 58; **4:** 47; **6:** 54
Comstock Lode (Nevada) **8:** *22*, 24
concordant coasts **6:** 44–46
conglomerate **2:** 40, *41*
conifers **3:** 55, 56, 57
constructive plate margins **5:** 11(*map*) *see* spreading plate boundaries
contact metamorphism **1:** 15; **2:** 52, 53
continental crust **5:** 9, 32
continental drift **5:** 16–21, 22
continental plate **5:** 10 *see also* tectonic plates
continental shelf **5:** 43
continental shields *see* shields
convection, convection cells **4:** 30–32; **5:** 10, 20
copper **1:** 29, 31, *31*; **8:** 1, 8, 21, 24, 25, 39
    native **1:** 31; **8:** *13*
    ores **8:** *13–15*
corals **3:** *18–20*, 52, 53, 54, 56, 57, 58, 59
    recognising fossils **3:** 20
cordillera **5:** 39
core (earth's) **1:** 6, 7; **4:** 20, 21; **5:** 6
Cornwall (England) **7:** 28; **8:** 24, 45
Cornwall (Pennsylvania) **8:** 25
corundum **1:** 23, *40*
Cotswold Hills (England) **6:** 34
*Crassatella* **3:** 30
crater **4:** 56, 57, 58 *see also* caldera
crater lakes **4:** *58–59*; **6:** 57
Crater Lake (Oregon) **4:** 58–59; **6:** 57
cratons **5:** 54; **7:** 25
Cretaceous, Cretaceous Period **3:** 50(*chart*); **5:** 20(*map*); **7:** 18(*name*), 21(*chart*), 50(*map*)–52; **8:** 36, 37
    fossils **3:** 58–59
    life **7:** 51
    rocks **7:** 51
crinoids **3:** *34–35*, 52, 53, 55
    recognising fossils **3:** 35
Cripple Creek (Colorado) **8:** 24
crocodiles **3:** 57
cross-bedding **2:** 35–37
cross-cutting, principle **7:** 8
crude oil **8:** 59
crushing, ores **8:** 54, 57
crust, earth's **1:** 7, 8; **4:** 20, 21, 30–31; **5:** 6, *7–9*
crustaceans **3:** 38
crustal plate *see* tectonic plate
crystal system **1:** 26–27
crystals **1:** 5
    crystallisation **1:** 12–13
    form **1:** 26–27
Cuba **5:** 38
cubic crystals **1:** 26
cubic zirconia **1:** 54
cuestas **6:** 34–35, 38, 39
Cumberland Plateau (United States) **5:** 45
Cumbria (England) **8:** 25
current bedding **2:** 35

cyclothem **2:** 50, 51

# D

dacite **4:** 39, 45
*Dactylioceras* **3:** 28, 56
Dartmoor (England) **7:** 39
Darwin, Charles **7:** 16
Death Valley (California) **1:** 45; **4:** 27, 28; **6:** 49
Deccan Traps (India) **2:** 24; **4:** 47; **5:** 58; **7:** 52, 56
deposit, deposition **6:** *15–17*
destructive plate boundaries **11**(*map*) *see* collision plate boundaries
detrital limestone **2:** 48; **3:** 20
Devil's toenail *see Gryphaea*
Devon (England) **7:** 38
Devonian, Devonian Period **3:** 50(*chart*); **7:** 18(*name*), 21(*chart*), 38–39; **8:** 37
    fossils **3:** *54*
    life **7:** 39
    rocks **7:** 39
diabase **2:** 27
diamond **1:** 23, 31, *32*; **7:** 51; **8:** 34
*Dicellograptus* **3:** 43
*Dictyonema* **3:** 42
*Didymograptus* **3:** 43, 53
dinosaurs **3:** 17, 46, 47, 56, 57, 58
    extinction **3:** 58
    footprints **3:** 11
    recognising fossils **3:** 47
    vertebra **3:** 46, 57
Dinosaur National Monument (Colorado/ Utah) **3:** 47; **7:** 49
diopside **1:** *57*
diorite **2:** 21, *26–27*
dip **6:** 32
dip slope **6:** 34, 35
*Diplodocus* **3:** 46
dipping rock strata, landforms **6:** 32–40, 43
    and petroleum **8:** 32
discontinuity **2:** 38
discordant coasts **6:** 44–46
distillation, fossil **3:** 11
dolerite **2:** 26, 27; **6:** 32
dolomite **1:** 18, 19, *45*; **2:** 13, 47; **7:** 42; **8:** 9
domes **6:** 40
    petroleum **8:** 32
Donets (Russia), coal fields **8:** 35
dragonflies **3:** 55
drift **8:** 46
Du Toit, Alexander **5:** 18, 19
*Dunkleosteus* **3:** 44
dykes **1:** 10, 12; **2:** 19; **6:** 52, 53, 56, *58*
dyke swarms **6:** 58

# E

earth, internal structure **4:** 20–21; **5:** 6–7
earthquakes **4:** *4–29*
    collision plate boundaries **4:** 17, 18
    global pattern **4:** 15(*map*)–19; **5:** 34(*map*)
    hot spots **4:** 17
    landforms **4:** 5, *22–29*
    measuring magnitude and intensity **4:** *10–12*
    spreading plate boundaries **4:** 17
East African Rift Valley **5:** 11, 30, 31, 58; **7:** 54, 56

East Pacific Rise **5:** 11, 26, 52; **7:** 55, 56
echinoderms (Echinodermata) **3:** *34–37*, 52, 53
echinoids **3:** *36–37*, 53, 56, 57, 58, 59
   irregular **3:** 36, 37
   recognising fossils **3:** 37
   regular **3:** 36, 37
El Misti volcano (Peru) **4:** 41; **7:** 59
electrolysis **8:** 57
element **1:** 5
*Elrathia* **3:** 41, 52
emerald **1:** 55
Eocene, Eocene Epoch **3:** 59
eons **3:** 50
epicentre **4:** *6*
epochs **3:** 50; **7:** 20
eras **3:** 50; **7:** 20
   naming **7:** 14–15
erosion **6:** *13–15*
eruption types, volcanic **4:** 46–57
   fissure-type **4:** 46–47
   Hawaiian-type **4:** 47–49
   Icelandic-type **4:** 46–47
   Pelean-type **4:** 50–51, 55
   Plinian-type **4:** 51, 55
   Strombolian-type **4:** 50
   Vulcanian-type **4:** 50, 53
Erzgebirge (Germany) **8:** 24
escarpments **6:** 34, 35
Euramerica **7:** 38, 40 see also Laurussia
Eurasian Plate **5:** 11, 50
eurypterids **3:** 38
evaporites **1:** 17, 18; **2:** 13, *51*; **8:** 27
Everest, Mount (Nepal/China) **5:** 43, 49;
   **6:** 13
exoskeleton **3:** 6, 38
extrusive rocks, extrusions **2:** *16–18*, 22–25

**F**

facies **3:** 14; **7:** 16
family (biol. classification) **3:** 16
fault plane **4:** *6, 7*
fault scarps **6:** 47–48
faults **4:** *6*; **8:** 32
   landforms **4:** 5, 23, 25, *26–29*; **6:** 5, 43,
   *47–51*
   lateral **4:** 26; **6:** 47 see also
   transcurrent faults
   normal **4:** 26, 28; **6:** 47
   reversed **4:** 26; **6:** 47
   thrust **4:** 26; **6:** 47
   transcurrent **4:** 26, 28–29; **6:** 47
   transform **4:** 26 see also transcurrent faults
*Favosites* **3:** *18*, 19
feldspars **1:** 17, 19, *50–51*; **2:** 10–11 see also
   orthoclase feldspar, plagioclase feldspar
*Fenestella plebeia* **3:** 17
ferromagnesian minerals **2:** 12
Fingal's Cave (Scotland) **4:** 47
fish **3:** 42, *44–45*, 53, 54, 58
fjord **7:** 59
flint **1:** 50; **2:** 34
flood basalts **2:** 24; **6:** 53,
flowering plants **3:** 55
fluorite **1:** 20, 23, *43*
focal depth, earthquake **4:** 6, 18
focus, earthquake **4:** *6*
fold axis **6:** 39

fold belts **5:** 44
folds, folding **2:** 8; **5:** 44, 50; **6:** 10, 37–40
   petroleum traps **8:** 32
foliation **2:** 58, 59
fool's gold **1:** 35, 37; **8:** 16
formations **7:** 7, 20
fossil fuels **8:** 7 see coal, petroleum, natural gas
fossilisation **3:** 5, 6–11
fossilised wood see petrified wood
fossils **3:** *4 AND THROUGHOUT*
   biological classification **3:** 16
   earliest known **3:** 51
   forming environments **3:** 11–8
   geological time **3:** 13–15, 50–59
fractionating tower **8:** 59
fracture zone **4:** *6*
fractures **6:** 19, 41
Frasch process (Herman) **8:** 51
Front Range, Rocky Mountains (United
   States/Canada) **5:** 42
frost shattering **6:** 22
froth-flotation process **8:** 53, 54
Fuji, Mount (Japan) **4:** 40
Fushun Basin (China), coal fields **8:** 36

**G**

gabbro **2:** 21, 27
galena **1:** *36–37*; **8:** 17
Ganges Plain (India) **6:** 11
gangue **8:** 9, 52, 53, 56
garnet **1:** 16, *52*; **2:** 12
garnetiferous schist **2:** 58
gastropods (Gastropoda) **3:** *32–33*, 52, 53, 54,
   56, 58, 59
   recognising fossils **3:** 32
gems **1:** 5
genus, genera (biol. classification) **3:** 16
geode **1:** 5, 49
geological column **3:** 50; **7:** 21
geological eon see eon
geological epoch see epoch
geological era see era
geological periods **3:** 50; **7:** 17, 18, 20
   names **7:** 17–18
geological systems **3:** 50; **7:** 20
geological time **7:** *4 AND THROUGHOUT*
geological time scale **7:** 14–59
   column *chart* **3:** 50; **7:** 21
   dating **7:** 19, 20, 21
   development **7:** 14–19
   divisions **3:** 50
   fossils **3:** 13–15, 50–59; **7:** 9
geosynclines **5:** 11, 29
Giant's Causeway (Northern Ireland) **4:** 47
glauconite **2:** 43
gneiss **1:** 17; **2:** *59*
   mining **8:** 44
goethite **1:** 40
gold **1:** 31, *32*; **7:** 35, 49, 51; **8:** 8, 10, *15*, 24,
   34, 38, 39, 57
   native **8:** *15*
   panning **8:** *39*
   rushes **8:** *40*
Gondwana **5:** 16; **7:** 30, 32, 34, 36, 38, 40, 41,
   42, 43, 46, 48, 50
*Goniatites globostriatus* **3:** 17, 27
goniatites **3:** 17, 26, 27
Goosenecks State Park (Utah) **6:** 29

gorges **6:** 29, 30
graben **4:** 27, 28; **6:** 48, 49
graded bedding **2:** 37–38
Grand Canyon (Arizona) **7:** *4–10*, 54
Grand Staircase (Arizona/Utah) **7:** *4–13*
granite **1:** 8; **2:** 10, 21, *28–30*; **6:** 18
   mining **8:** 44
granodiorite **2:** *30*
graphite **1:** 21, 31, *33*
graptolites **3:** 53, *42–43*, 52, 53
   recognising fossils **3:** 42
gravel, mining **8:** 7, 44
greywacke **2:** 44
Great Basin **5:** 39, 42; **7:** 53
Great Dyke of Zimbabwe **7:** 25, 27
Great Glen Fault (Scotland) **6:** 50
Great Plains/High Plains (United States)
   **5:** 39, 42
Great Slave Lake (Canada) **7:** 24
Greenland **7:** 58
greensand **2:** 43
gritstone **2:** 43
grossular garnet **1:** 52
groundmass **1:** 20
groups (geol. classification) **7:** 20
*Gryphaea* (Devil's toenail) **3:** 31
guard, belemnites **3:** 25
Gulf of Mexico, oil fields **8:** 37
Guyana Shield **5:** 56
gypsum **1:** 19, 23, 27, 28, *46*; **2:** 13

**H**

haematite **1:** 21, 29, *41*, 42; **8:** 11, *16*
Half Dome, Yosemite National Park
   (California) **2:** 30; **6:** 5, 59
halide minerals **1:** *43*
halite **1:** 18, 19, 29, *43*; **2:** 13, 51 see also salt
*Halysites catenularius* **3:** 17
Hamersley Basin (Australia) **8:** 26
Hamersley Range (Australia) **5:** 56; **7:** 23
*Harpoceras* **3:** 27
Harrisburg (Pennsylvania) **6:** 37
Hauy, Rene Just **1:** 30
Hawaiian Islands **5:** 4, *58–59*; **6:** 9; **7:** 54, 57
Hayward Fault **5:** 53
headlands **6:** 41, 43
heart urchins **3:** 36, 37
Hell's Canyon (Idaho) **2:** 15
*Hemiaster* **3:** *36*, 37
*Hemicidaris* **3:** 37
Herculaneum (Italy) **4:** 51
Hercynian Mountain Building Period **7:** 41
Hercynian Mountains **5:** 45; **7:** 30
Hess, Harry **5:** 27
hexacorals **3:** 18, 19
hexagonal crystals **1:** 26, 27
High Force Waterfall (England) **6:** 32
Himalayas, Himalayan Mountains **5:** 4, 11, 36,
   43, *48–51*, 44; **6:** 10, 13; **7:** 54, 56
hogback **6:** 34, 35
Holmes, Arthur **5:** 19; **7:** 19
Holocene Epoch **7:** 58
hornblende **1:** 14, 16, *57*; **2:** 12
hornblende granite **2:** 29
hornfels **1:** 15; **2:** *55*
horst **4:** 27, 28; **6:** 48, 49
hot spots **4:** 47; **5:** 54, *58–59*; **7:** 57
   earthquakes **4:** 17

Hutton, James **5:** 14; **7:** 16
hydraulic action **6:** 41
hydrothermal concentration of minerals
　　　**8:** 22–26
hydrothermal deposit **1:** 13
hydrothermal veins and zones **1:** 11; **8:** 24
hydroxide minerals **8:** 53
hypocentre **4:** *6*

# I

Iapetus Ocean **7:** 30, 35, 37
Ice Age **5:** 17; **7:** 53, 58
ice wedging **6:** 22
Iceland **4:** 46; **5:** 11, 27, 29,
ichthyosaurs **3:** 46, 57
*Ichthyosaurus quadriscissus* **3:** 46
igneous rocks **2:** 9, *14–31,* 21*(table)*
　　　mineral forming environments **1:** 8, *9–14*
　　　ores **8:** 20–25
ilmenite **1:** *41;* **8:** 9
imprint, fossil **3:** 9, 10
index fossils **3:** 57, 58
Indian Ocean **7:** 53, 55, 57
Indian Shield **5:** 57
indium **8:** 11
Indo-Australian Plate **5:** 11
Indus River (Pakistan) **6:** 15
inner core, earth's **5:** 6
*Inoceramus* **3:** 31
insects **3:** 10, 38, 55, 56
intrusive rock, intrusion **2:** 16, *19–20, 26–31*
invertebrate **3:** 6
ions **1:** 5
iron **8:** 8, 11, 25, 33, 34, 54, 55
　　　ore **1:** 41
　　　pyrite *see* pyrite
　　　native **8:** 16
　　　ores **8:** *16,* 26, 27
　　　smelting **8:** 54–55
island arcs **5:** 24, *34–35*
Isle of Arran (Scotland) **6:** 58
Isle of Skye (Scotland) **6:** 26
isostacy **5:** 57; **6:** 10, 14

# J

Jacks Mountain (Pennsylvania) **6:** 37
jade, jadeite **1:** 57
Jamaica **8:** 33, 27, 36
Japan, Japanese Islands **5:** 34
jasper **1:** *50*
jellyfish **3:** 51
joints, in rocks **2:** 37; **6:** 18–21, 41
Juan de Fuca Plate **5:** 11, 39
Juan de Fuca Ridge **5:** 52
Juniata River (Pennsylvania) **6:** 37
Jura Mountains (Switzerland/France) **5:** 44,
　　　51; **6:** 37, 38
Jurassic, Jurassic Period **3:** 50*(chart);*
　　　**5:** 19*(map);* **7:** 17*(name),* 21*(chart),*
　　　*48(map)–49*
　　　fossils **3:** 57–58
　　　life **7:** 49
　　　rocks **7:** 49

# K

Kaikoura Mountain Building Period **7:** 57
Kalahari Desert (Southern Africa) **5:** 55
Kalgoorlie (Australia) **8:** 24

Kambalda nickel deposit (Australia) **8:** 21
Kamchatka Peninsula (Russia) **5:** 33, 35
Kazakhstania **7:** 30, 34, 36, 40, 42
Kenya, Mount (Kenya) **5:** 30
Kermadec Islands (New Zealand) **5:** 35
Kilauea (Hawaii) **4:** 42, 49, *57;* **5:** 59
Kilbarri National Park (Australia) **7:** 37
Kilimanjaro, Mount (Tanzania) **5:** 30
Kimberley (South Africa) **1:** 32, 53
kimberlite **1:** 32; **7:** 51
King Island (Australia) **8:** 25
kingdom (biol. classification) **3:** 16 *see* bivalves
Kirkland Lake (Australia) **8:** 24
Kiruna, Sweden **8:** 22
Kodiak Island (Alaska) **4:** 22
Kun Lun Shan (China) **5:** 4
Kurile Islands (Japan/Russia) **5:** 34
Kuroko deposits **8:** 26
Kuznetsk Basin (Russia), coal fields **8:** 36
kyanite **1:** 27, *53*

# L

labradorite **1:** *51*
laccolith **6:** 52, 53
Lake Superior (United States) **8:** 26
Lake Tahoe (California) **5:** 40
Laki fissure (Iceland) **4:** 46
lamellibranchs (Lamellibranchiata) **3:** 24 *see*
　　　bivalves
landforms **6:** *4 AND THROUGHOUT*
　　　effect of rock structure at coasts **6:** *41–46*
　　　effect of rock structure on land **6:** *26–40*
　　　from dipping beds of rock **6:** *32–40, 43*
　　　from earthquakes **4:** 5, *22–29*
　　　from faulting **6:** *47–51*
　　　from folded beds of rock **6:** *32–40*
　　　from horizontal beds of rock **6:** *26–32,*
　　　　　34
　　　from igneous activity **6:** *52–59*
landslide **5:** 5, 7, 22, 23, 55
Laramide Mountains **7:** 30
laterite **8:** 33
Laurasia **5:** 19; **7:** 42, 44, 48, 50
Laurentia **7:** 30, 32, 34, 36, 39
Laurussia **7:** 38, 41
lava **2:** 16, 17; **4:** 35, 37; **6:** 52, 53, 55
　　　bombs *see* volcanic bomb
　　　flows **4:** 37, 41, 49
　　　plateaux **6:** 52
　　　tubes **4:** 48
law of superposition **7:** 14
Le Puy (France) **2:** 19; **6:** 56
lead **1:** 22; **8:** 8, 10, 24, 25
　　　ores **8:** 17
　　　smelting and refining **8:** 56, 57
Lehmann, Johann **7:** 14
*Leptograptus* **3:** 43
Lesser Antilles **5:** 38
Lewistown (Pennsylvania) **6:** 37
lignite **8:** 28, 29, 36*(map)*
limestone **2:** 47–49; **3:** 7, 20
　　　landforms **6:** 17, 23, 24, 25, 34, 37
　　　mining **8:** 7, 44
　　　use in smelting **8:** 55, 57
limonite **1:** *41*
*Limulus* (king crab) **3:** 38
*Lingula* **3:** 22, 52
lithosphere **5:** 7, 8, 9

Llallagua (Bolivia) **8:** 24
Loch Ness (Scotland) **6:** 50
lode **8:** 24
lodestone **1:** 42; **5:** 21; **8:** 16
Los Angeles **4:** 13; **5:** 52
Love waves **4:** 8
Lower Carboniferous **3:** 55; **7:** 40
L waves *see* Love waves
*Lycopod* **3:** 48, 55
Lyell, Charles **7:** 17

# M

Mackenzie Dyke (Canada) **7:** 25
magma **1:** 9; **2:** 19; **4:** 31–32, *34–35,* 36
magma chamber **1:** 10, 11; **4:** 34, 40, 58; **6:** 14,
　　　52, 53
　　　minerals **8:** 20–25
magnesium **8:** 8, 11
magnetic stripes **5:** 25–26
magnetite **1:** *42;* **8:** *16*
malachite **1:** 20, *45;* **8:** *13*
Malham Cove (England) **6:** 24
Malvern Hills (England) **6:** 34
mammals **3:** 42, 56, 57, 59
mammoth tooth **3:** 59
manganese **8:** 8, 11
　　　ores **8:** *17*
mantle, earth's **1:** 6, 7; **4:** 18, 20; **5:** 6, *9*
marble **2:** *57*
　　　mining **8:** 7, 44
marginal accretion **5:** 55
Mariana Islands **5:** 34
Mariana Trench **5:** 11, 33
mass extinction **3:** 52, 53, 54, 55, 56, 57, 58,
　　　59
Matterhorn (Switzerland/Italy) **5:** 50
matrix **1:** 51; **2:** 20, 41; **3:** 20
Mauna Loa (Hawaii) **4:** 43, 48, 49; **5:** 59
Mayon, Mount (Philippines) **4:** 40
Mazama, Mount (Oregon) **4:** 59
McArthur River (Australia) **8:** 25
mercury **8:** 10
Merensky Reef (South Africa) **8:** 21
Mesa Verde National Park (Colorado) **7:** 52
mesas **6:** 26, 27, 34
Mesozoic, Mesozoic Era **3:** 50 *(incl. chart);*
　　　**7:** 15*(name),* 21*(chart),* *44–45*
　　　fossils **3:** 56–59
　　　life **7:** 45
metals, metal ores **8:** 7, *12–19*
metamorphic aureole **8:** 45
metamorphic rocks **2:** 9, *52–59*
　　　mineral forming environment **1:** 8, *14–
　　　17*
meteorites **7:** 23, 24
micas **1:** 14, 16, 58; **2:** 11 *see also* biotite and
　　　muscovite
*Micraster* **3:** 36, 37, 58
Mid-Atlantic Ridge **5:** 11, 25, 27; **7:** 56
Middle East, oil fields **8:** 37
　　　rift valleys **5:** 30, 31
mid-ocean ridges **5:** 11, 24, 25, 27
millerite **8:** 18
millipedes **3:** 38, 54
mineral forming environments **1:** *4–19*
mineralisation of fossils **3:** 5, 7

minerals **1:** *4 AND THROUGHOUT see also* ores, ore minerals
  classification **1:** 31
  cleavage **1:** 25 *see also* slaty cleavage
  colour **1:** 20–21
  fracture **1:** 25
  habit **1:** 28
  hardness **1:** 22–23
  identification **1:** 20–29
  lustre **1:** 22
  naming **1:** 31
  specific gravity **1:** 24
  streak **1:** 21
  translucence **1:** 24, 25
  transparency **1:** 24, 25
  twinned crystals **1:** 28
Minesota Mine (Michigan) **1:** 31; **8:** 13
mining **8:** 7, *38–51*
  hill and valley mining **8:** 40, 42,
  long-wall **8:** 47
  open pit **8:** 40, 42–43
  quarrying **8:** 7
  room-and-pillar **8:** 44, 46–47
  solution **8:** 51
  stone quarrying **8:** 44
  strip **8:** 41
  surface **8:** 40–44
  underground **8:** 44–51
Miocene, Miocene Epoch **3:** 59; **5:** 21*(map)*; **7:** 55*(map)*
Mississippian **3:** 55; **7:** 40
Modified Mercalli Scale **4:** 10–12
Mohs' Scale of Hardness **1:** 22–23
Mohs, Frederick **1:** 22
molluscs (Mollusca) **3:** 24–33, 52, 54, 55, 56, 58, 59
mould, fossil **3:** 9, 10, 40
molybdenite **1:** *37*; **8:** 17
molybdenum **8:** 8, 10, 25
  ores **8:** *17*
monoclinic crystals **1:** 27
*Monograptus* **3:** 43, 53
Monument Valley (Arizona/Utah) **6:** 26, 27
moonstone **1:** 28
Moorea (French Polynesia) **4:** 43
Morenci Mine (Arizona) **8:** 14
mosasaurs **3:** 58
Mount Isa (Australia) **8:** 25, 52
mountain belt **5:** 10
mountain building **6:** *6–12*
mountain building period **7:** 35, 41, 45, 48, 54, 57
mountain limestone **7:** 40, 41
mountain root **5:** 8
Mountains of the Moon National Monument (Idaho) **4:** 44
mudstone **2:** *45–47*
Murchison, Roderick **7:** 18
muscovite **1:** 16, 25, *59*; **2:** 11 *see also* mica
mussels **3:** 29, 30
*Mya* **3:** 30
*Mytilus* (mussel) **3:** 30

**N**

nappes **5:** 50
Narryer, Mount (Australia) **7:** 24
native elements, metals, minerals **1:** *31–34*; **8:** 9, *10*, 13, 15, 16, 18, 20, 22, 24, 34, 39

Natural Bridges National Monument (Utah) **7:** 43
natural gas **8:** 30, 32, 36*(map)*
Nazca Plate **5:** 11, 36, 38
needle rocks, at coast **6:** 45
  on land **6:** 27
*Neuropteris* **3:** 49, 55
Nevadan Mountain Building Period **7:** 45, 48
New Madrid (Missouri), 1812 earthquake **4:** 12, 17
New River Gorge (West Virginia) **7:** 40
Niagara Escarpment **6:** 30; **7:** 36
Niagara Falls (United States/Canada) **6:** *30–32*; **7:** 36, 37
nickel **8:** 10, 18, 21, 24
  ores **8:** *18*
NiFe zone **1:** 7
North American Cordillera **5:** *39–42*
North American Plate **5:** 11
North Island (New Zealand) **5:** 35
North Sea, oil fields **8:** 37
Northridge 1994 earthquake **4:** *13–15*
nuée ardente **4:** 50 *see also* pyroclastic flow

**O**

Oak Ridge Fault (California) **4:** 13
obsidian **2:** *22*; **4:** 39
ocean crust **5:** 9, 22, 24, 25, 26, 27, 32
ocean floor, characteristics **5:** *22–24*
  spreading **5:** 25 *see also* spreading plate boundaries
ocean plate **5:** 10 *see also* tectonic plates
ocean ridges, oceanic ridges *see* mid-ocean ridges
oceans, formation **7:** 24–27
ocean trenches **5:** 4, 24, 27, 34
*Ogygenus* **3:** 40, 53
oil, crude oil **8:** 7, 30, 31, 32, 36*(map) see also* petroleum oil
oil fields *see* petroleum fields
oil shales **2:** 46; **8:** 32, 50
Ojos del Salado (Argentina/Chile) **5:** 38
Old Red Sandstone **7:** 38, 39
Oligocene Epoch **3:** 59
olivine **1:** 14, *53*; **2:** 12
Olympic Mountains (Washington) **5:** 39
onyx **1:** *50*
ooliths, oolitic limestone **2:** 47, 48
opal **1:** *50*
order (biol. classification) **3:** 16
Ordovician, Ordovician Period **3:** 50*(chart)*; **7:** 18*(name)*, 21*(chart)*, *34(map)–35*; **8:** 37
  fossils **3:** 53
  life **7:** 35
  rocks **7:** 35
ore minerals **8:** *8–19 see also* ores
ores **8:** 7, *8 AND THROUGHOUT*
  formation and location **8:** *20–37*
  igneous rocks **8:** *20–25*
  mining **8:** *38–51*
  processing and refining **8:** *52–59*
  sedimentary rocks **8:** *26–37*
organic rocks **2:** 32
orogenic belt *see* mountain belt
orogeny *see* mountain building period
orpiment **1:** 21
Ortelius, Abraham **5:** 14
orthids **3:** 22

orthoclase feldspar **1:** 14, 16, 23, *51*; **2:** 10 *see also* feldspars
*Orthonota* **3:** 30
orthorhombic crystals **1:** 26, 27
orthosilicate minerals **1:** *52–54*
ossicles **3:** 34, 35
*Ostrea* (oyster) **3:** 30, 31
outcrop **6:** 32
outer core **5:** 6
overburden **8:** 39
oxide minerals **1:** *39–42*; **8:** 11, 53

**P**

Pacific Ocean **5:** 26, 39; **7:** 48, 50, 55, 57
Pacific Plate **5:** 11
Pacific Ring of Fire **7:** 56
Paget, François **5:** 15
pahoehoe lava **2:** 17, 24; **4:** 37, 44
Palaeocene Epoch **3:** 59
palaeomagnetism **5:** *21–26*
Palaeozoic, Palaeozoic Era **3:** 50 *(incl. chart)*; **7:** 15*(name)*, 21*(chart)*, *28–31*
  fossils **3:** *52–56*
  life **7:** 30
  rocks **7:** 31
Pangaea **5:** 18*(formation)*, 22, 56; **7:** 42, 43, 44, 46, 48, 50
*Paradoxides* **3:** 40, 52
Paricutin (Mexico) **4:** 44
Parke's process **8:** 57
peat **8:** 28
*Pecten* (scallop) **3:** 29, 30
*Pectoperis* **3:** 49
pedicle, in brachiopods **3:** 20, 21, 22
pegmatites, pegmatite veins **1:** 13; **2:** *31*; **8:** 20
Pelecypoda **3:** 29 *see* bivalves
Pelée, Mount (Martinique) **4:** 50
pelycosaurs **3:** 56
Pennsylvanian **3:** 55; **7:** 40
pentlandite **8:** 18
period *see* geological period
permeable rock **8:** 31
Permian, Permian Period **3:** 50*(chart)*; **5:** 18*(map)*; **7:** 18*(name)*, 21*(chart)*, *42(map)–43*; **8:** 36, 37
  extinction **3:** 56
  fossils **3:** *55–56*
  life **7:** 43
  rocks **7:** 43
Persian Gulf **8:** 37
Peru-Chile Trench **5:** 11, 36
Petrified Forest National Park (Arizona) **3:** 8; **7:** 47
petrified forest **3:** 7, 8
petrified wood **3:** 7, 8, 48
petroleum **8:** *30, 36(map)*
  drilling **8:** 48–49
  fields **8:** 31–32, 37, 48–50
  formation **8:** *30–32*
  location **8:** *37*
  oil **7:** 47, 51
  refining **8:** *58–59*
  reservoirs **8:** 31–32
  traps **8:** 31–32
*Phacops* **3:** 1, 40, 54
Phanerozoic Eon **3:** 50; **7:** 28
phenocrysts **2:** 20, 29
Philippine Islands **5:** 34, 35

Philippine Plate **5:** 11
phosphate minerals **1:** 47
phragmacone **3:** 24, 25
phyllite **2:** 55–56
phylum (biol. classification) **3:** 16
Pico de Teide (Tenerife) **4:** 58; **5:** 23
Pilbara Shield (Australia) **7:** 25
pillars 46: 1,
pillow lava 41
Pine Point (Canada) **8:** 25
Pinotubo, Mount (Philippines) **4:** 51
pitching folds **6:** 39
placer deposits **1:** 17, *18*; **8:** 33–35
plagioclase feldspar **1:** *51*; **2:** 10 *see also* feldspars
planetismals **7:** 22
plants **3:** *48–49*, 51, 53, 54, 55, 56, 57, 59
plate boundaries **5:** 28–53
plate tectonics **5:** *4 AND THROUGHOUT*
    fossils and **5:** 15
    theories and evidence of **5:** *12–27*
plateaux **6:** 26, 27, 52
platinum **1:** 31, *33*; **8:** 10, *18*, 21
    native **8:** *18*
playa lake **1:** 17
Pleistocene Epoch **7:** 57*(map)*, 58
plesiosaurs **3:** 46, 57, 58
Pliocene Epoch **3:** 59
plug *see* volcanic plugs
plunging folds **6:** 39
plutonic rocks **1:** 10, 14; **2:** 26
Pompeii (Italy) **4:** 51
porphyry, porphyritic rock **2:** 17, 20; **8:** 24
potash **8:** 51
potash feldspar *see* orthoclase feldspar
Potosí (Bolivia) **8:** 24
Precambrian, Precambrian time **3:** 50*(incl. chart)*; **7:** 21*(chart)*, *22–31(incl. map)*; **8:** 26
    fossils **3:** 51–52
    life **7:** 26
    rocks **7:** 25
Primary Era/Period **7:** 15*(name)*, 28
primary seismic wave *see* P wave
primary waves *see* P waves
primates **3:** 58
Prince William Sound (Alaska) **4:** 22, 23, 24, 25
*Priscacara liops* **3:** 45
prismatic crystals **1:** 29
processing and refining ores **8:** *52–59*
productids **3:** 22, 55
Proterozoic Eon **7:** 25
*Psilophyte* **3:** 48
pteridophytes **3:** 48
pterosaurs **3:** 46, 57, 58
*Ptychagnostus* **3:** 52
Puerto Rico **5:** 38
pumice **1:** 12; **2:** 17, 23
P waves **4:** *8*, 20, 21; **5:** 7
pyrite **1:** 20, 25, 26, 29, 35, *37–38*; **3:** 9, 11; **8:** 9, *16*
pyrite dollar **1:** 35
pyroclastic flow **4:** 37, 54, 55
pyroclastic rocks **2:** *18*; **4:** 37
pyrolusite **1:** *42*; **8:** 17
pyroxenes **1:** 56; **2:** 12; **4:** 38
pyrrhotite **8:** 18

## Q

quartz **1:** 14, 16, 19, 23, 25, *48–49*; **2:** 11
Quaternary, Quaternary Period **3:** 50*(chart)*; **7:** 15*(name)*, 21*(chart)*, 57*(map)*, *58–59*
    life **7:** 59

## R

radioactive dating **7:** 19
Rainier, Mount (Washington) **4:** 42; **7:** 56
*Raphidonema faringdonensis* **3:** 58
Rayleigh waves **4:** 8
razor shells/razor clams **3:** 29, 30
Red Sea **5:** 11, 30, 31; **7:** 54
refining **8:** 53, 54, 57–59
regional metamorphism **1:** 15; **2:** 52, 53
reptiles **3:** 42, *46–47*, 55, 56, 57, 58, 59
    recognising fossils **3:** 47
reservoir rock **8:** 31
resources, geological **8:** *4 AND THROUGHOUT*
Rhine Gorge (Germany) **7:** 38, 39
rhynconellids **3:** 23
rhyolite **2:** 21, *22*; **4:** 38, 39
ria **7:** 59
Richter Scale **4:** *10–12*
Richter, Charles F. **4:** 10
rifts, rifting, rift valleys **4:** 24, 27–28; **5:** 24, 29, 30, 31; **6:** 48–49
ring silicates **1:** *54–55*
ripples **2:** 35, 37
risers **6:** 28
roasting **8:** 53, 54, 55
rock cycle **2:** 6–8; **6:** *4–17*
rocks **2:** *4 AND THROUGHOUT*
    landforms **6:** 18 *AND THROUGHOUT*
    minerals **1:** 4; **2:** 10–13
    oldest intact **7:** 24
rock salt **2:** 51
Rocky Mountains, Rockies (United States/ Canada) **5:** 39, 40, 41; **7:** 30, 31, 39, 52, 53
rose quartz **1:** 22
ruby **1:** 29
rudists **3:** 58
rugose corals **3:** 18, 19, 20, 53, 56
rupture, rupture zone **4:** 6, 7
rutile **1:** *42*

## S

Saint Helens, Mount (Washington) **4:** 36, 45, 51, *52–56*; **5:** 39
salt (sodium chloride) **2:** 13; **8:** 27, 28 *see also* halite
    mining **8:** 44, 51
salt domes **8:** 32, 51
San Andreas Fault (California) **4:** 13, 17, 28, 29; **5:** 11, *52–53*; **6:** 51; **7:** 53, 57
San Fernando Valley (California) **4:** 13, 14
San Francisco (California) **4:** 17, 19, 29; **5:** 52, 53
    1906 earthquake **4:** 9, 12, 29
sand dollar **3:** 37
sand mining **8:** 7, 44
sandstones **2:** 42–44; **6:** 20, 21, 27, 35, 37; **8:** 44
scale trees *see* Lycopod
scallop **3:** 30
scarp slope **6:** 34, 35

schists **1:** 16; **2:** 57, *58*
scleractinian corals **3:** 56, 58
scoria **2:** 17
    cones **4:** 44
sea urchins **3:** 36
seamounts **4:** 43
Secondary Era/Period **7:** 15
secondary waves *see* S waves
Sedgwick, Adam **7:** 18
sediment, sedimentary deposition **2:** 33–38; **6:** 15–17
sedimentary mineral forming environments **1:** 8, *17–19*
sedimentary rocks **1:** 17; **2:** 9, *32–51*
    minerals in **1:** *19*
    ores **8:** 26–37
seed bearing plants **3:** 48, 54, 56
seed ferns **3:** 55
segregation **8:** 21
seismic gaps **4:** *18–19(map)*
seismic waves **4:** *6–10*, 20–21
seismogram **4:** 8
seismograph **4:** 8
selenite **1:** 28
series, rock **3:** 50; **7:** *20*
serpentine **1:** 59
    mining **8:** 44
serpentinite *see* serpentine
shadow zone (P and S waves) **5:** 7; **4:** 20, 21
shaft **8:** 39, 46
shales **2:** *45–47*; **6:** 20, 13, 34, 37
Shark Bay (Australia) **7:** 26
sharks **3:** 44, 54, 59
sharks' teeth, fossils **3:** 6, 45
shear waves *see* S waves
sheet silicate minerals **1:** *58–59*
sheeting, in rocks **6:** 18, 19
shields (continental shields) **5:** *54–57*; **7:** 25
shield volcanoes *see* volcanoes
Ship Rock (New Mexico) **6:** 56
SiAl zone **1:** 7
Siberia **7:** 30, 32, 34, 36, 40, 41, 42
Sierra Nevada batholith **6:** 59
Sierra Nevada Mountains **5:** 39, 40; **7:** 45, 53
Silesia (Russia), coal fields **8:** 35
silica **4:** 35, 38
    mineral replacement **3:** 9
    unit **1:** *47*
silicate minerals **1:** 7, *47–59*; **8:** 11, 53
silicon **1:** 7
sills **1:** 10, 12; **2:** 19; **6:** 52, 53, *59*
Silurian, Silurian Period **3:** 50*(chart)*; **7:** 18*(name)*, 21*(chart)*, *36(map)–37*
    fossils **3:** 53
    life **7:** 37
    rocks **7:** 37
silver **1:** 31, *34*; **8:** 8, 10, 22, 24, 25, 57
    native **1:** *34*; **8:** 10
SiMa zone **1:** 7
siphuncle **3:** 26
skarns **8:** 25
slates **1:** 16; **2:** *55–56*
    mining **8:** 7, 44
slaty cleavage **2:** 56
smelting **8:** 53, 54, 55–56
Smith, William **7:** 16
smithsonite **8:** *19*
smoky quartz **1:** 6; 20, *48*

Snider-Pellegrini, Antonio **5:** 14
Snowy Mountains (Australia) **5:** 45
South America **5:** 36
South American Cordillera **5:** 36
South American Plate **5:** 11, 36, 38
South Island (New Zealand) **5:** 35
Southern Alps (New Zealand) **5:** 35; **7:** 57
spatter cone **4:** 49
species **3:** 16
sphalerite **1:** 25, *38*; **8:** *19*
*Sphenophyllum* **3:** 49
*Sphenopteris* **3:** 49
spicules **3:** 52
*Spirifer bollandensis* **3:** 54
spiriferids **3:** 22, 54
Spitzbergen (Norway), coal fields **8:** 36
sponges **3:** 51, 52, 54, 58
spreading plate boundaries **5:** 28, *29–31*
stacks, sea stacks **6:** 41–46
staircases **2:** 4; **6:** 28–29
*Stapellella* **3:** 41
starfish **3:** 36
staurolite **1:** *53*
*Stegosaurus* **3:** 57
Steno, Nicolaus **1:** 30; **7:** 14
stibnite **1:** 29, *38*
Stillwater Dyke (Montana) **7:** 25
stipes, graptolites **3:** 42, 43
stocks **6:** 52, 53
stratigraphy **7:** 4
stratovolcanoes *see* volcanoes
stratum (strata) **2:** 32; **7:** 4
striated crystals **1:** 29, 55
strike, direction of **6:** 32
stromatolites **3:** 48, 51, 52; **7:** 26
Stromboli (Italy) **4:** 50
Strutt, John **7:** 19
stumps, coastal **6:** 45 43, 45, 46
subduction, subduction zones **5:** 10, *29*, 32–34
Sudbury, Sudbury Igneous Complex (Canada) **1:** 35; **8:** 21
Suess, Eduard **5:** 16
sulphate minerals **1:** *46*
sulphide minerals **1:** *35–38*; **8:** 10–11, 34, 35, 53
sulphur **1:** 20, 31, *34*; **8:** 25, 26
    mining using Frasch process **8:** 51
surface waves **4:** *8,* 10 *see also* Rayleigh waves, Love waves
Susquehanna River (Pennsylvania) **6:** 36, 37
sutures, ammonoids **3:** 26, 27
S waves **4:** *8,* 10, 20, 21; **5:** 7
syncline **6:** 37, 38, 39
system *see* geological systems

## T

tablelands **6:** 27, 34
tabular crystals **1:** 29
tabulate corals (Tabulata) **3:** 18, 19, 20, 53, 56
Taconic Mountain Building Period **7:** 35
Taiwan earthquake **4:** 5, 16
talc **1:** 23, *59*
tar sands **8:** 50
Tasman Geocycline **7:** 39
Taylor, Frank **5:** 16
tectonic plates **4:** 30, 31, 32, 33; **5:** 9
terebratulids **3:** 22, 23

Tertiary, Tertiary Period **3:** 50(*chart*); **7:** 21(*chart*), *55–57*; **8:** 36, 37
    fossils **3:** 59
    life **7:** 56
    rocks **7:** 57
Tethys Geosyncline **7:** 45, 47
Tethys Ocean **5:** 48, 49, 51; **7:** 43, 44, 45, 46, 48, 49, 50, 53, 55
tetragonal crystals **1:** 26
*Tetragraptus* **3:** 43
Texas oil fields **8:** 31, 50
therapsids **3:** 56
Tibetan Plateau **5:** 4, 43, 50; **7:** 56
Tien Shan (China/Russia) **5:** 50
tillite **5:** 12, 16
tin **8:** 11, 24, 34, 38, 39
    mine **8:** *45*
    ores **8:** *18*
titanium **8:** 8, 11
Titusville (Pennsylvania) **8:** 50
Tonga **5:** 35
topaz **1:** 23, *54*
tourmaline **1:** *55*
trails, fossils **3:** 11
transform (scraping) plate boundaries **5:** 28, *52–53*
traps **2:** 24
treads **6:** 28
trees **3:** 55
trellis drainage pattern **6:** 36
trenches *see also* ocean trenches
Triassic, Triassic Period **3:** 50(*chart*); **7:** 18(*name*), 21(*chart*), *46(map)–47*; **8:** 36
    fossils **3:** 56–57
    life **7:** 47
    rocks **7:** 47
triclinic crystals **1:** 27
trilobites **3:** 6, 15, *39–41*, 51, 52, 53, 54, 55, 56
    recognising fossils **3:** 39
trona **8:** 51
tsunami **4:** 22, 23
tuff **2:** 18, *25*; **4:** 38
tungsten **8:** 25
*Turitella* **3:** 32
Turkey, earthquakes **4:** 16
*Tyranosaurus rex* **3:** 46, 58

## U

unconformity **7:** 8; **8:** 32
uniformitarianism, principle **7:** 11
Upper Carboniferous **3:** 55; **7:** 40
Ural Mountains (Russia) **7:** 30, 39, 41
uraninite **1:** *42*
uranium **8:** 11, 24

## V

vale **6:** 35
valve **3:** 21, 29
vanadium **8:** 21
veins **8:** 20, 24 *see also* hydrothermal veins
Venezuela **5:** 38
Vermillion Cliffs (Arizona/Utah) **7:** 5, 10, 12
vertebrates (Vertebrata) **3:** 6, *42–46*, 53
vesicles **2:** 16
Vesuvius, Mount (Italy) **4:** 51
Vishnu Formation/Vishnu Schists **7:** 6, 7, 8
volcanic ash **2:** 16, 18, 19; **4:** 35, 36; **6:** 24, 55

volcanic bombs **2:** 18; **4:** 35, 36
volcanic cone **6:** 52, 53, 55
volcanic eruptions *see* eruptions
volcanic glass **2:** 17 *see also* obsidian
volcanic landforms **6:** *53–59*
volcanic plugs **2:** 19; **6:** 52, *55–56*
volcanic rocks **4:** *37–39 see also* extrusive rocks
volcanoes **4:** *30–59*
    active **4:** 34
    central vent **4:** 40
    collision plate boundaries **4:** 32, 33
    complex **4:** 40
    composite **4:** 40
    dormant **4:** 34
    eruption violence **4:** 45
    extinct **4:** 34
    seamounts *see* seamounts
    shapes **4:** 40–45
    shield **4:** 42–43, 48, 57; **6:** 53
    spreading plate boundaries **4:** 32, 33
    stratovolcano **4:** 38, 40, 41–42; **6:** 55
    world distribution **4:** 33
Vulcano (Italy) **4:** 50

## W

wacke **2:** 44
water gap **6:** 36
Waterton-Glacier International Peace Park (Montana/Canada) **7:** 33
weathering **2:** 39; **6:** *22–25*
    and climate **6:** 25
    chemical **2:** 40; **6:** *23–24*, 25
    ferromagnesian minerals **2:** 12
    mechanical **2:** 39; **6:** *22*
    minerals **8:** 34
Wegener, Alfred **5:** 16, 18, 19, 20,
Wenlock Edge (England) **7:** 37
Werner, Abraham Gottlob **1:** 30
Whitby (England) **7:** 44
White Cliffs of Dover (England) **7:** 52
Whitney, Mount (California) **5:** 40
wind gap **6:** 34, 36
Witwatersrand (South Africa) **8:** 34, 40

## Y

Yellowstone National Park (Wyoming) **1:** 19; **5:** 58
Yilgarn Shield (Australia) **7:** 25
Yorkshire Dales (England) **8:** 25
Yosemite Valley, Yosemite National Park (California) **5:** 40; **6:** 4, 5, 19, 59; **7:** 44

## Z

Zagros Mountains (Turkey/Iran) **6:** 12
zeolite minerals **1:** *52*
zinc **8:** 8, 10, 11, 24, 25, 57
    ores **8:** *19*
    smelting **8:** 56
zinc blende **8:** 19
Zion Canyon (Utah) **7:** 5, 10
zircon **1:** 26, *54*; **7:** 24